SIMPLE SERMONS
FOR THE
MIDWEEK SERVICE

BOOKS BY THE SAME AUTHOR

SIMPLE SERMONS FOR THE MIDWEEK SERVICE

by

W. Herschel Ford, B.A., D.D.

ZONDERVAN PUBLISHING HOUSE
Grand Rapids, Michigan

CONTENTS

FOREWORD

From time unknown the midweek church service has been called, simply "the prayer meeting." I have always called this service "The Sweetest Hour of the Week." My dear friend, Dr. John E. Huss, calls it "The Hour of Power."

Truly the midweek service can be a sweet hour of prayer and power. Many churches look upon this hour as a spiritual stepping stone between Sundays, but sad to say, many churches have done away with this service. Their people are the losers because of it.

I hope that my preacher brethren can and will use these simple messages as an aid to building a strong spiritual midweek service in their churches. A little later I hope to have another such volume published, entitled "*More Simple Sermons for the Midweek Service.*"

W. HERSCHEL FORD

7061 Old Kings Road, South
Apartment 49
Jacksonville, Florida, 32217

SIMPLE SERMONS FOR THE MIDWEEK SERVICE

1.

Christians in the Wrong Places

I John 2:15-17

Christians are not perfect people. We know we are not, the world knows it, God knows it. Someday, when Jesus comes to take us to be with Him, we shall be perfect for we shall be like Him. But we'll not be rid of our imperfections until that glorious day. Jesus, in His great sermon, said, "Be ye therefore perfect, even as your Father which is in heaven is perfect" (Matthew 5:48). That's the goal, that's the ideal toward which we are always striving. We are never to give up. If we are not striving toward perfection, we are sorry Christians, indeed. We must aim at the moon, even if we hit the streetlight.

I have flown many times over the mighty Mississippi River. As I have looked down upon it I have noted that its course is always in a southward direction. Sometimes it flows eastward, westward or even northward, but the general trend of the river is in a southward direction. So, although the Christian sometimes goes in the wrong direction, although he often sins, the definite trend of his life is upward and Godward. He is going on toward perfection.

But the Christian often gets into the wrong places. I am not now speaking of physical places, but of mental and spiritual places. Let us think of several of these places, using a scriptural example to illustrate each of them.

I. SOME CHRISTIANS GET UNDER THE TREE OF DISCOURAGEMENT

Elijah, the Old Testament prophet, is our example here. He had just won a mighty victory. You will remember the contest he waged with the prophets of Baal on Mt. Carmel. Two altars were built with an offering to be made upon each altar. Elijah and these false prophets were to pray to their gods, pleading

11

that their particular god would send down fire to consume their
respective offerings. The God who sent down the fire would be
declared the true God. The prophets prayed all the day long
and nothing happened. Then Elijah offered a short prayer and
God answered with fire. The flames leaped all over the offering,
consuming not only the sacrifice, but the wood, the stones and
the water in the trench surrounding the altar. You see, God
never does anything in a halfway manner.

When this happened the great crowd shouted, "The LORD, he
is the God; the LORD, he is the God" (I Kings 18:39). Then the
false prophets were put to death. It was a great day of victory
and exultation. Now when the news reached the ears of Jezebel,
the wicked queen, she was violently angry. She sent a message
to Elijah, "You've slain my prophets;" she said, "I'll do the same
to you. By this time tomorrow you'll join them in death."

What did Elijah do when he received this threat? He forgot
how God had been with him. He forgot how God had given
him the victory. He forgot how God had protected him. And
he started running. He didn't stop running until he reached
Beersheba and when he got there, exhausted and frightened,
he sat down under a juniper tree. All he could think about was
Jezebel's threat and in despair he asked God to let him die.

It's mighty easy for us to get under that tree today. We become discouraged so easily, we forget that God cares for us, we
forget the blessings of the past, we forget how God has brought
us out of our troubles on other occasions. Oh, how we worry
about this thing and that thing, instead of looking up to God for
help. He always has been with us. He always will be. Why
can't we trust Him? He cares for the lilies of the field and
not a sparrow falls without His knowledge.

There is a wonderful word for us in *Isaiah 26:3*, "Thou wilt
keep him in perfect peace, whose mind is stayed on thee. . . ."
There's our trouble, when difficulties arise we look at the trouble
instead of looking up to God. But we dishonor Christ when we
sit under the tree of discouragement. We tell the world that
He can't do much for us, we tell them that our religion isn't
of much help in time of need. So let's get out from under
that tree and out into the open fields of faith where we can
look up and see His face.

II. Some Christians Get Up on the Housetop of Self-Ease

One day David the King was idling on the roof of his palace. The battles were over, he had nothing to do. And temptation came to him in the form of a beautiful woman. He fell before that temptation, and in doing so broke at least four of God's ten commandments. Thus the man after God's own heart, the man who had been so close to God, tore his soul out of fellowship with God.

Someone has said that "an idle brain is the devil's workshop." How true! David was tempted when he was not busy for God. Many Christians are on that same housetop of self-ease. They are contented merely to have their names on the church roll, they are satisfied to be nominal church members. In the light of Christ's sacrifice, the salvation He has given us, the blessings He has bestowed upon us, no Christian ought to be satisfied if he is doing nothing for the Lord.

A life of self-ease shrivels the soul. As rust corrodes metal, self-ease and inactivity corrode the soul. The soul cannot grow without some spiritual nourishment. Every Christian ought to keep on growing. He ought to know more of the Lord and the Bible and God's work now than he did a year ago, and much more than he did five years ago. Yet some are content to remain as babes in Christ.

The church affords many means of spiritual growth and we can find additional means in our private devotions. Yet too many Christians take their Christian responsibilities too lightly. For example, we hear so many trifling excuses, "I couldn't come to church because it was raining." "I couldn't come because we had company. I had a headache. My wife wasn't feeling too good." None of these things keep you from your work on Monday — why do you permit them to keep you from church on Sunday?

The life of self-ease often causes Christians to drift into sin. It brought about David's downfall. I have known many Christians who were active and faithful members of their home church, then they moved to another city and failed to move their church membership. Some of them would say, "I'm going to rest for a while." And soon they were drifting, soon the world had engulfed them and they were doing things they had never dreamed they would do. If they had been busy for the Lord, this never would have happened.

The Christian is a man of divine privileges, but with privileges come responsibilities. Let us assume our responsibilities as readily as we accept our privileges. Let's climb down off the housetops of self-ease and get busy for Christ.

III. SOME CHRISTIANS GET INTO THE DOUBTING CASTLE OF UNBELIEF

John the Baptist was a mighty man of God. He came preaching a flaming gospel and the crowds heard him and responded. Then he was arrested and placed in a prison. As he languished in his cell day by day doubts began to gnaw at his soul. He said, "I wonder if this Man was really the Christ, or do we look for another?" Have you ever been in Doubting Castle? Maybe you said, "I wonder if it's all true. I wonder if the Bible is God's Word. I wonder if I have really been saved, I wonder if there is anything to the Christian religion after all."

Now doubt cools our love. If you love a person and begin to doubt him, your love soon cools off. And when you doubt Christ and the Bible your love for Him cools off. And most of all He wants us to love Him.

Then doubt dampens our zeal. When a man believes in a thing he gives his best to it. For instance, I believe that God called me to preach and I believe in the whole Gospel. So I will try to preach that Gospel as long as I live. If I doubted my call and the truth of the Bible and the power of the Gospel, my zeal would soon wane and die.

Do you have some doubts about spiritual things? Then take out your heart and hold it up in the light of His love. Remember all that He did and said. Remember all the experiences you have had with Him, remember all the answered prayers. Then when you see the truth in these things and the reality of Christ and what He has done for you, come out of Doubting Castle.

IV. SOME CHRISTIANS GET INTO THE RING OF WRANGLING

The disciples did not seek the lowest places nor those places closest to the Saviour. No, they wanted prestige and position, they sought the highest places. Then on one day Christ found them disputing about who would have the highest position. So He gave them a lesson in opposites. He said that the one who would be highest must first be lowest, that the one who would be greatest must first be the servant of all.

Most church quarrels start after such wrangling. Someone wants the high place, someone wants the entire church to go his way. Oh, we need men and women who will take any place for Christ. We grieve the Spirit of God when we wrangle. Get out of that ring and serve God wherever you can and you'll find happiness and success.

V. SOME CHRISTIANS GET INTO THE SIEVE OF SELF-CONFIDENCE

Simon Peter is our example here. When Jesus prophesied that cruel men would put Him to death Peter said, "No, Lord, they'll have to kill me first." He was so very self-confident. But Jesus recognized that his boasting was of the flesh, so He said, "Satan is going to sift you like wheat and you are going to fall." And he did, he denied Jesus three times. When he was sifted and tried, his self-confidence failed him.

When a Christian gets all puffed up, when he thinks too highly of himself and his works, that is just the time when Satan grabs him. In other days I knew a young man who was being widely used as an evangelistic singer. It seems that the notice given him rather turned his head, for one day he said to me, "I am not really as great as these preachers think I am." He didn't last long in the Lord's work. Before many months he was out of the work and living a very worldly and sinful life.

When we think that the work we are doing for the Lord is successful because of us, our talents, our work, our brilliance, we are certainly riding for a fall. We must remember that it is all of God, we must not trust too much in our own strength. Paul spoke of it this way, "I have planted, Apollos watered; but God gave the increase" (I Corinthians 3:6). It matters not how much we do, how hard we work, if God is not in it, our efforts are as tinkling brass and a sounding cymbal.

The poet says, "Let self be crucified and slain and buried deep." It must always be that way with us. Self must be put out of the way and Christ must be preeminent.

VI. SOME CHRISTIANS GET ON THE SLIPPERY PATH OF WORLDLINESS

Lot is our example here. He and his uncle Abraham had separated. Lot chose to live in the wicked and worldly city of Sodom. But he lost more than he gained. His wife and daughters soon were deep in the swim of society and Lot himself almost forgot God. The city fathers gave him a prominent position and it meant more to him than the things of God. Lot went down and down until he lost his home and his married daughters. His wife was turned into a pillar of salt and his single daughters sank into deepest sin.

Too many Christians are like Lot. They get mixed up with the world. With one hand they try to hold on to the church and with the other they hold on to the world. Before long they give up the things of God and give all to the things of the world. Let the Christian be warned that the world is after him. Often when a Christian is active in the church, the world marks him out as a capable person and goes after him, offering him a position that will bring him some worldly recognition. And too many Christians fall for it.

There is no sweet fellowship with God on the slippery path of worldliness. It's hard to pray there. Do you pray on the dance floor or at a card party? Can you witness there for Christ? Then when you get on your knees to pray and know that you are allowing the things of the world to come between you and God, you just can't pray as you should.

A preacher and a young lady were talking about the matter of dancing. She insisted that her worldliness did not affect her Christian testimony. The preacher asked her if she could witness for Christ on the dance floor. She assured him that she could. So the preacher said, "Suppose you try it the next time you are at a dance." The young lady agreed to do so. In the middle of a dance she said to her partner, "Are you a Christian?" He said, "No, I am not. Are you?" She answered, "Yes," whereupon her partner said, "Then what are you doing here?" That's the way the world feels about a Christian who is on the slippery path of worldliness.

Then there is no spiritual power on that pathway. The world saps the Christian's power and causes him to lose his influence. I John 2:15 says, "Love not the world, neither the things that are in the world. If any man love the world, the love of the Father is not in him." Let the Christian have a good time, but let it be in the right way. Get your joy from the best things in life and not the lowest. If we could get our church members to give as much time and energy to the Lord's work as they do the world, we would have the strongest churches on earth.

VII. Some Christians Become Ensnared in the Meshes of Disobedience

Moses had been faithful for many years, then there came a careless moment. God told him to speak to the rock and water would come out. But Moses was angry with the people. He wanted to show them his power so he struck the rock. As a result he lost the Promised Land. When we disobey God we lose many Promised Lands.

For instance there is the matter of the Lord's Supper, which we are to observe often in remembrance of Christ, even as He commanded. Yet many of our people go for years without obeying this direct command. God wants every Christian to serve Him. ". . . ye are not your own, For ye are bought with a price . . ." (I Corinthians 6:19, 20). The only happy Christian life is the obedient life.

God may not call you to preach or occupy some prominent position, but He does call you to give Him your best wherever you are. Too many people are wasting the only life they'll ever have. An artist spent many years modeling a group of figures. But when the figures were finished he could not get them out of the room to carry them to the exhibition. He felt that his time was wasted. Let's not waste our time on the things that we can't enjoy in eternity. Let us lay up our treasures in heaven.

When I was a boy a man brought his balloon to our little town for an exhibition flight. The balloon was soon filled with the gas that would cause it to rise, but it did not rise. Why? Because it was chained to the ground. Then some men released the chains and the balloon and the man soared high into the sky. Oh, let us not permit the world to chain us down. Let's strike off these worldly shackles and rise up to serve our Master.

One day a man was converted on the Damascus Road. He was blinded for three days, then God sent a messenger to say to him, "You will suffer many things for Christ's sake." And suffer he did as no man has ever suffered for Christ. But when he came to the end of the way he could say with assurance, ". . . there is laid up for me a crown of righteousness, which the Lord, the righteous judge, shall give me at that day . . ." (II Timothy 4:8). Yes, and there's a crown for us, too, if we'll be faithful to our great God and Saviour, Jesus Christ.

2.

People Our Church Could Do Without

Philippians 3:15-21

This may seem to be a harsh subject to some. You may say, "We need every member we have. Great tasks lie ahead and we need the help of everyone." That is true, we need the help of everyone whose heart is right and who wants to help out in the Lord's work. But there are some people that the church would be better off without. Paul said in his day that there were some who lived in such a manner as to be enemies of the cross. If one is an enemy of the cross he is an enemy of the church, and the church would be better off without such enemies.

I hope that none of you comes under this heading. If so, I pray that before you sleep tonight you will get right with God and man and become the person the church needs, a person whose life glorifies God. Now let us think of some of those whom the church could do without.

I. THE CHURCH COULD DO WITHOUT THOSE WHOSE LIVES ARE SINFUL

They bring reproach upon the church, they testify to the world that Christ and the church have done nothing for them. If you have your name on the church roll and you are living in sin, you are hurting the church. The outsider wants an excuse for not being a Christian, he wants to justify himself. So he measures himself by the church member who is not living a good life and says, "I am as good as he is, so I guess I'm all right."

We are the only gospel the sinner will read. They don't look for Christ in the Bible or in the world of nature, but they do look for Him in our lives. If they see sin there instead of Christ the church is hurt. Christ said, "You are my witness." What is a witness? He is one who testifies in behalf of another. When a

18

man is on trial a lawyer puts up a character witness to testify for his client and his case is benefited by it. Well, Christ needs witnesses and the best ones are those whose lives testify to His saving grace. But if there is sin in your life your testimony counts against Christ and His church.

Here is a man who boasts that he is a church member. But in business he puts over a shady deal, at the cocktail party he drinks like anyone else, on the golf course he uses profanity and bets on the game. He is not a good witness, his life hurts the cause of Christ.

Fit a cork tightly in a bottle and throw the bottle in the ocean. Not a drop of water will get in the bottle. And if a man has sin in his life, he can come to church every Sunday, but no blessing will enter his heart. He won't get a blessing himself nor can he bring a blessing to anyone else. So I say that the church would be better off without those whose lives are sinful. I know that no church member is perfect, but at least many of them are trying to live a good life.

II. THE CHURCH COULD DO WITHOUT THOSE WHO STRIVE FOR THE HIGHEST POSITIONS

Nothing is so obnoxious as politics within the church, with the members jockeying for position and prestige. Some who are not able to receive that recognition quit the church in a "huff." It's easy to sing, "Where He leads me I will follow." But often those who sing that song refuse to take a small place in the church. They want the big place or none at all.

Let me give you a contrasting picture. During the depression I assumed the pastorate of a church where a prominent doctor served as superintendent of the Sunday school. He said to me, "Pastor, if you want to make a change, it will be entirely agreeable with me. I will work anywhere you put me." And he really meant it. . . . Some years later I became pastor of another church. One day I had lunch downtown with the Sunday school superintendent of that church. We had just called an educational director to serve the church. The Sunday school superintendent said to me, "Pastor, it would be best for our new educational director to serve as Sunday school superintendent. I want you to know that I love the Lord so much that if you want me to sweep the church and scrub the floor I will do it."

And I said to myself, "What a great spirit! We can build a wonderful church with men like that."

Five years went by and this man gave very little cooperation. Then one night in a committee meeting he got up and told how I had thrown him out of the superintendent's place when I came there as pastor. He hadn't meant what he said about sweeping the church and scrubbing the floor. For five years this thing had rankled in his heart. All he wanted was the recognition. Such people never help a church.

St. Augustine said, "There are four articles in the Christian's creed. The first is humility, the second is humility, the third is humility, the fourth is humility." Once I asked one of the women in our church why a certain Mrs. A. did not attend the meetings of the Woman's Missionary Union. She answered, "She attended when she was the president, but since she is no longer in that position she does not attend." Are such people interested in the cause of Christ or simply in some high position?

Jesus said, "He that would be greatest of all, let him be the servant of all." The way up is down. Do your best for God in a little spot and you won't have to worry about promotion.

III. The Church Could Do Without Those Who Indulge in Destructive Criticism

There is constructive criticism and there is destructive criticism. When one man feels there is something wrong in the church he calls some of the other members aside and harshly criticizes. That is destructive criticism, the kind the devil likes. But another man, having the same feeling, keeps quiet about it. Then he goes to the pastor or some other leader and talks it over in a sweet Christian spirit and they pray about it. That is constructive criticism and it leaves no scars.

It seems that some people are in the church, not for a blessing, not for help, but to find something they can criticize. A man said to me once, "I am the chief critic in my church." And I said, "I don't want you in my church, then — we have enough critics now."

The church is not perfect, the pastor, the deacons, the staff, the choir members, none of these is perfect. But neither are you. Why go around talking about the splinter in someone else's eye when you have a big piece of timber in your own? No, we are not perfect, but we are doing our best for the Lord and His church. Are you?

Some people are happy to work for the Lord while others love to criticize them. It is a dangerous thing to criticize the church. You would not like for someone to criticize your child who is dear to you. Well, the church is the dearest thing on earth to Christ. When you criticize it you are not pleasing Him and He will not hold you guiltless.

A certain man was accustomed to forming quick opinions. He saw a certain girl every day, although he had never met her. He said, "I don't imagine she ever gives a thought to sacred things." Later he saw her in action and she proved to be a deeply dedicated, consecrated Christian. He said, "I've learned my lesson. I must not criticize so readily, I may not know all the facts." That's a good lesson for us all.

IV. The Church Could Do Without Those Who Say "It Can't Be Done"

The church is no place for pessimism. We have a great God and a great mission. He has promised to help us in all we do for Him, so we ought to be Christian optimists!

Here is a great building going up. Two groups of men are there. One group is working, the other group stands on the sidelines, saying, "It can't be done." One day the building is finished and the worker is rewarded, while the knocker stands aside and scowls. The church is a great spiritual building and every one of us can have a part in its work. At the end of the year some can say, "I had a part in the record of my church this year." Others must say, "The church had a great year but I did nothing to help." At the end of the way there is a crown of reward for the builder, there is nothing for the knocker.

V. The Church Could Do Without The Mean, Selfish, Stingy People

Isn't it a pity that a man who has been bought by the blood of Christ and saved from hell, can be mean and little and stingy with his church? Lord, give us big people, people with big spirits, people who rise above pettiness.

A man is a nonentity who takes all that the community gives and gives nothing in return. It's true also in the church. Some people seem to have as their motto, "Me first, myself next, and if there is anything left I'll take it."

Some time ago I saw a double cartoon. The first picture showed a man buying some theater tickets. The price was shown at $5.00 each and up. He said, "Give me the best in the house." The other picture showed the same man in church on Sunday morning. The offering plate was being passed by him and he scowled as he dropped in a dime. His favorite song must have been: "When we asunder part it gives us inward pain."

A man has a right to the good things of life that he has worked for, a nice home, a color TV, some summer trips, an up-to-date automobile. But he has no right to acquire these things at the expense of God's tithe. Yet that's just what he is doing when he isn't giving God His part of his income.

A homespun philosopher once wisely said, "You can buy your furniture on the extortion plan, but you can't get to heaven on a nickel a week." We don't need "nickel nursers," but people whose pocketbooks have been converted. Real good Christians are big, broad, liberal people.

VI. The Church Could Do Without Lazy People

An ox and a mule worked together. One day the ox decided that he wouldn't work, so he stayed in the barn. That night he said to the mule, "Did the boss say anything about my not working today?" And the mule answered, "No, he didn't say anything about your not working, but he had a long talk with the butcher on the way home."

Even God can't use lazy people. Check the Bible and you'll find that He called only the busy people into His service. Lazy folk are the castaways of the Kingdom of God. *Proverbs 19:24* says, "A slothful (lazy) man hideth his hand in his bosom, and will not so much as bring it to his mouth again." What a picture of a man who is even too lazy to feed himself.

Some people are too lazy to get up on Sunday morning and go to church, some are too lazy to attend prayer meeting. They are too lazy to do anything for God or for others. You can never grow a great church on lazy people.

VII. THE CHURCH COULD GET ALONG
WITHOUT GOSSIP-MONGERS

It seems that we have these people always with us. They gladly pick up a little gossip, roll it over under their tongue a few times, enlarge it and send it on its way. They never check to ascertain the truth, they just send the gossip rolling. In a town where I was pastor there was a woman who had the reputation of having the longest tongue in the community. She came to one of my deacons one day and said, "I wish you would make the pastor stop preaching about gossip." Now I had not preached about gossip. I had just preached the Gospel and she felt guilty and pointed out her own sin.

Well, suppose we know one who has done wrong. What should be the Christian attitude to exhibit? Should we be silent or should we tell someone else about it? Let's see what the Word of God says. "Brethren, if a man be overtaken in a fault, ye which are spiritual, restore such an one in the spirit of meekness; considering thyself, lest thou also be tempted" (Galatians 6:1).

The word "restore" here has the meaning of a resetting, like the resetting of a bone which is done by a skillful surgeon. So when a person does wrong we are to seek to restore him, to get him back in the right place. We are to restore and not tear down, we are to pull up and not push down.

VIII. THE CHURCH COULD DO WITHOUT
OVERLY-SENSITIVE PEOPLE

There are some people who are mature in age, who are supposed to have good sense, yet we are forced to "walk on pins and needles" lest we say something that will hurt their feelings. You can say the same thing to a thousand people and it will be all right with nine hundred and ninety-nine, but the other one will swell up, get his feelings hurt and become angry.

Do you know Brother and Sister Hurtfeeling? I have known hundreds of them. A woman said to me, "I can't get my husband to go to church. His feelings were hurt in church when he was a boy." Many persons who ought to be serving the Lord are doing nothing because their feelings were hurt 25 years ago. What a shame! When they get to heaven Christ will say to them, "Why didn't you serve Me?" And they'll say, "Lord, I got my feelings hurt." And surely when they see the prints of the nails in His hands, they will be filled with shame.

IX. The Church Can Get Along Without Unfaithful People

You see a death notice in the paper which reads like this: "Mr. A. B. Jones died Tuesday afternoon. Funeral services at 10 A.M. on Thursday. He was a member of the First Baptist Church." And you say, "That's certainly a surprise to me. I never saw him at church, he never gave a dime, he never took a stand for Christ." And his church membership card is taken from the active file and placed in the file marked "deceased." The church never misses him. After all, when you lose nothing you miss nothing.

The way to be a good witness is to be faithful. Most people cannot preach or teach or sing in the choir. But every single one of us can be faithful. That's where God's reward comes in. *Revelation 2:10* ". . . be thou faithful unto death, and I will give thee a crown of life."

Two brothers fought side by side in World War I. In a fierce battle one of them was wounded and lay in No-Man's Land. His brother begged the captain for permission to go out and get him, but the captain said, "No, you would probably be killed." "But he expects me to come out," replied the soldier. "All right, go ahead," said the captain. The man crept out and pulled his brother back into the trench. The captain said, "I told you it was of no use. He is dead, you see." "Yes sir," said the soldier, "but he was still alive when I reached him and when I crawled up beside him he said, 'Tom, I knew you would come, I just felt sure you would come.' I did what he expected of me and I would have been ashamed if I hadn't."

Christian, someone is expecting something of you — your pastor, your friends, your Saviour. He is expecting you to do your best for Him. Then when He sees you at the end of the way it will be worth it all to hear Him say, "My child, I counted on you and you didn't disappoint Me."

3.

People Our Church Could Not Do Without

Philippians 4:1-7

Paul organized many churches and his interest in them never ceased. This was only natural. Some of these churches pleased him, some of them disappointed him. It seems that the church at Philippi was his favorite. In the text he calls the members of that church ". . . my brethren dearly beloved and longed for, my joy and crown, . . . my dearly beloved (Philippians 4:1). He felt that the church at Philippi represented the crowning work of his life, and of course, it brought him his greatest joy.

There are some people in every church like these Philippian Christians. They are a crown of joy to the pastor, they make his life worthwhile, they cause his heart to swell with joy. The church could not get along without them. Who are they? Let us think of their practical qualifications.

I. The Church Could Not Get Along Without Faithful People

The Bible nowhere commends anyone for greatness or brilliance, but for faithfulness. "Well done, thou good and faithful servant . . ." (Matthew 25:21) is the plaudit given by the Master.

Let me give you a contrasting picture of two men who were members of one of my churches. One man was a lawyer, a judge, a college graduate, a brilliant man. But he attended church only about once a month. He would come and make a great speech to a Sunday school class, and everyone thought he was wonderful. We gave him a class of men to teach and he started off in a great way. But he could never be counted on to be present. Soon he resigned his position. Although he was a talented and well-educated man, he meant very little to his church. The other man was a janitor in a bank, a man of limited

25

education. But he was always at church, he gave his tithe each week, he invited others to church and sought to win them to Christ. Because he was faithful the janitor's life counted more for God than the life of the brilliant judge!

In 1927 Lou Gehrig of the New York Yankees was the outstanding baseball player of the year. He deserved the honors showered upon him because he was faithful. During his lifetime he played in more consecutive games than any other man in the history of the sport. He never missed a game. They called him the "Iron Man of Baseball." When he died a movie was made of his life with the title, "The Pride of the Yankees." What made Lou Gehrig great? It was his faithfulness. Every day he was out there on first base doing his best. Now if Christ picked out the most outstanding member of our church, who would it be? It would surely be the one who was most faithful.

In 1912 the *Titanic* went down in the Atlantic Ocean. It was said that as the ship began to sink the band was playing, "Nearer My God to Thee." The band members stuck to their post and went down to their death. Jesus said, ". . . be thou faithful unto death, and I will give thee a crown of life" (Revelation 2:10). Yes, there are crowns here and hereafter for the faithful Christian.

So my prayer is, "God give us faithful Christians." We need people who are faithful in giving, faithful in attendance, faithful in consecrated Christian living, faithful in service, faithful in witness. We couldn't get along without faithful people, we can't have too many of them.

II. THE CHURCH COULD NOT DO WITHOUT WILLING PEOPLE

Oh, we have some willing people, all right, some willing to work and others willing for them to do it! Then we have so many members who are willing to do the work of the world, but not the work of the Lord. The club calls them, the lodge calls them, the outside organization calls them, and they are ready and willing. The Lord calls them, the church calls them, and they are "too busy." A man said to me, "I don't come to church on Sunday night because that's the only time I have for my family." Why? Because he gave the other nights to his social life and pleasures. Now he felt that he could give God's night to the family. Christians ought to be willing to make some adjustments, the church and the Lord ought to have priority. These other things will die with the setting sun, the things of Christ will last forever.

The grasshopper on the fence makes more noise than the ox in the field. But the ox does the work. Some people talk much but do nothing for the Lord. A good watch can be adjusted to five different positions and it will run well in any of these positions. But a clock is not so adjusted and will work well in only one position. Some folks work well anywhere in the church, others must have the preferred place. Others, those who really love the Lord, say, "Any place that I can serve suits me. It doesn't have to be a big place, I'm willing to work anywhere that I can glorify God and serve His cause."

III. The Church Could Not Do Without
People of Vision

We need first a vision of the needs about us. All around us there are unsaved and unchurched people by the hundreds. Many of them could be brought in if our people went after them seriously.

Then we need a vision of worldwide needs. Jesus said, ". . . Lift up your eyes, and look on the fields; for they are white already to harvest" (John 4:35). We must take care of the local needs but we must not stop there, we are to look to the regions beyond.

In 1835 the Primitive Baptists split off from the Missionary Baptists. They were called "Hardshells." They didn't believe in missions or schools or an educated ministry. They said, "If God wants to save people, He can do it without our help." But the Missionary Baptists said, "We believe in Christ's Great Commission, we will try to send the Gospel to the ends of the earth." What has been the result of these two opposing philosophies? The Primitive Baptists are almost gone, they have only a handful of struggling churches left in the country. On the other hand, the Missionary Baptists have grown into the millions. Their great churches are everywhere and their missionaries girdle the globe. What a revealing illustration! "He that would find his life must lose it." No church or group of people can grow by keeping the good news of the Gospel to themselves.

IV. The Church Could Not Do Without
Optimistic People

"We can't do that," some people say. "We have never done that before," some say. "God helping us, we will do that," the optimists say.

Moses was leading Israel toward the Promised Land. They came to the point where they could easily enter the land and settle down. God said to Moses, "Pick out twelve men, send them into the land. Have them look it over and bring you a report, then prepare to enter it." The twelve went in, found the land to be fertile and prolific and wonderful beyond description. Ten of the men came back to make their report. "It's a good land all right," they said, "but the men of the country are giants. We were like grasshoppers in their sight." The other two, Caleb and Joshua, said, "This is all true, but God is on our side and with His help we can take the land." The pessimists won out, which meant that Israel had to wander in the wilderness for forty long years.

And so today the difficulties of life are great and our enemies are many. But God is on the side of those who serve Him. He is stronger than all the outward circumstances. God and one are always a majority.

V. The Church Could Not Do Without
Industrial People

Jesus was industrious. He said, ". . . My Father worketh hitherto, and I work" (John 5:17). He filled every hour with good service to God. As you read through the Bible you find that God never used a lazy person. Moses and Noah and David and John the Baptist and Peter and Paul were all men of an industrious nature. They were workers.

The heads of a great corporation sit down and map out a big campaign. But that is not enough, they must have industrious workers to carry out their plans. The church has a great program, mapped out by the Lord Himself. But He needs industrious Christians to carry out His work. He has no hands but ours to do His work, no feet but ours to run His errands. If the work of the church is left to the lazy people, the church will die.

VI. THE CHURCH COULD NOT DO WITHOUT
ITS BOOSTERS

One of my deacons in a small town where I was pastor ran a department store. As he wrapped the packages and received payments from his customers, he always invited them to church. He was able to get more people to church than all of my other members put together. He was a booster.

We need boosters, we need people who are out every day, in every walk of life, telling others of the good times to be had in our church. Soon they would know that we had something worthwhile here for them. I like the slogan seen on some doors, "Come in without knocking, go out the same way." Remember that if you knock the church you are knocking yourself, for you are the church. If you want your church to grow and prosper, boost it!

VII. THE CHURCH COULD NOT DO WITHOUT
LIBERAL PEOPLE

Who are the liberal people? The one who gives a dollar per week may be, but the man who gives one hundred dollars per week may not be. We must measure a man's generosity by what he has left over. When a millionaire gives $50,000, we say he is liberal. But he still has $950,000 left over and he will not suffer financially. But a poor man who gives $5.00 and has only $1.00 left over, may be making a real sacrifice.

Years ago a certain rich man gave $780.00 per week to his church. His gifts were spoken of in many quarters. But he had a big store left over, a car and chauffeur, a lovely home. In my membership at the same time there was a washerwoman who gave seventy-five cents per week. If she happened to be sick, she would send in her gift. Somehow I believe that her gift was greater than that of the rich man, but nothing was said about it.

One day Jesus was sitting by the treasury. Some men came by and dropped in their large gifts, and they gave them in such a way that everyone could see the gifts. Probably someone said, "Did you see how much Mr. Abraham gave? My, he must love the Lord very much to give such a gift." Then a little woman, a widow, slipped in some small coins. She was probably very sorry that she could not give more. Nothing was said about her gift. But Jesus, who saw the woman and her gift, made her forever famous. He said, "She hath given all that she had." He measured her gift by what she had left over.

A penny and a dollar were talking as they lay together in the cash drawer. The dollar was boasting of how much it could do in the world. Then the penny said, "Yes, but I'm sure I go to church more often than you do." A man went into a drug store across the street from a church and said to the clerk, "Will you please give me change for a dime?" The clerk replied, "Yes, and I hope you enjoy the sermon."

If you love the Lord you need not be afraid of giving too much. He will always outgive you. It is not what you have but what you are that determines the amount of your gifts. Churches seem to get along without rich people, but they can't get along without liberal people.

At one time in its early history the Southern Baptist Theological Seminary was in dire financial straits. Three great preachers and professors were working hard to keep the school going. Finally one of them said in despair and grief, "I guess we'll just have to let the seminary die." But one of the others said, "Brethren, if the seminary is to die, let us die first." And with that attitude and by the giving of themselves in sacrificial service, the school was saved. Thousands of preachers and Christian workers have been trained in its classrooms and the seminary lives on.

That's the way we need to love our church. Let's give it the best we have, saying, "If it dies, let us die first." Then I'm sure we will have a church that pleases God and blesses hundreds of people.

4.

Does It Really Pay to Be a Christian?
I Timothy 4:8

Ever since man was created he has been asking the question, "Does it pay?" He considers a new job and asks, "Does it pay?" He considers an investment and asks "Does it pay?" He thinks of moving to another city and he asks, "Does it pay?" This question is asked by the student, the capitalist, the banker, the professional man, by the mechanic, the farmer, by all men.

Here is a young man just finishing high school who has an opportunity to go to college. He thinks of four years of study and hard work and he wonders if it would not be better to take a job instead. So he asks, "Will it pay?" A business man has a proposition presented to him and with pencil and paper he sits down to find the answer to the question, "Will it pay?" We don't usually ask how much good such a deal would do for others nor what contribution it would make to society. We are inherently selfish and so we ask, "Will it pay? What's in it for me?"

Well, what about Christianity? It is life's greatest undertaking. Does it really pay to give up your sin and come to Christ and live the Christian life? There are many motives for becoming a Christian, the love of God, the desire to do good, the longing to serve God and others. But most of us become Christians because we believe it pays. Christ has what we need. We need forgiveness, peace, hope and everlasting life. And when we come to Him He supplies all our needs. We come to know that it really pays to follow Christ.

Paul had been a Christian for many years and one day someone must have asked him if it had been a paying investment. And out of the years of experience we hear him saying, "Yes, it pays to serve Jesus, it is profitable for this life and the life that is to come." And every person who has faithfully tried Christianity and has followed Christ will come to the same conclusion.

31

I. It Pays to Be a Christian From the Physical Standpoint

This does not mean that when you become a Christian all of your diseases and physical troubles will disappear and that you will immediately become stronger and healthier. But it means that a Christian will live a cleaner life, he will treat his body better, he will conform to the principles of life which bring better health.

One man goes to bed at night and gets a good night's sleep. Another man stays up until after midnight, drinking and carousing and getting drunk. He has an awful "hang-over" the next morning, while the first man, a Christian who does not indulge in such things, wakes up fresh and feeling fine. The life that many unsaved people live is simply not conducive to good health.

Sin undermines health. Hundreds die before their time because of sin. A prominent surgeon came to Boston University to perform a certain operation. The medical students looked down from the surrounding balcony watching every movement of the great surgeon and listening to every word. Soon the doctor stopped for just a minute and said, as he looked up at the students, "Young men, three years ago, if this man had changed a certain habit, this operation would not have been necessary. One year ago a simple operation would have saved him. Now the verdict is very uncertain." And the young men came to realize the tragedy of a life of sin.

If all epitaphs were true some of them would say, "Here lies a man who died before his time because a sinful habit cut him down." Dr. Cyrus Edson, a famous New York physician, said, "A vicious person contains in his body the seeds of destruction. The Christian is best fitted to withstand disease and live a healthy life."

II. It Pays to Be a Christian From a Financial Standpoint

This does not mean that you are going to get rich simply because you are a Christian. In fact, most Christians are not wealthy. But it does mean that the Christian will not waste his money on sinful things, but on the better things of life. Think of those who uselessly and foolishly spend their money on whiskey and tobacco. Good Christians don't have that expense.

America's liquor bill now amounts to about thirteen billion dollars per year. (Not millions but billions!) Think of all the schools and hospitals and churches and childrens' homes and homes for the aged this money could build. Think of all the poverty that could be relieved with this money. But it is all wasted, it does no one any good.

Christ never wasted anything. After feeding several thousand people He said to the disciples, "Gather up the fragments." And they picked up twelve baskets full of food. He never wasted anything.

1. *Christianity pays off financially in the home.* The Christian man doesn't throw his money away on sin, thus causing his family to suffer. He brings his money home and uses it for the benefit of his family. A woman from a very modest home told me that her husband spent $90.00 per month on whiskey, money needed by the family. Because the Christian doesn't use his money in that manner, his family is better off.

When I was growing up in a little Southern town, I had a boy friend whose father was an excellent carpenter. He made good money but he spent it on drink. He always received his salary on Saturday nights and on many of these Saturday nights I would go with this boy and his mother, following the man up and down the street and into the stores, trying to get a little money from the man for groceries before he spent it all on liquor. It was a sad and pitiful situation. Now the real Christian is saved from such sorrow.

A man who had been a drinking man was gloriously and wondrously converted. One morning his wife said to him, "Which suit are you going to wear today?" And the dear man, with tears in his eyes, said, "Thank God you can ask me 'which suit.' This is the first time I have had more than one." Yes, it pays financially to be a Christian.

Out of my memory of years ago there comes the picture of a man who was an habitual drunkard and whose family suffered because of it. Then someone brought him to hear me preach. He came back again and again and one night he walked down the aisle and gave his heart to Jesus. That settled the sin question — there was no more drinking. And a year later this man's wife said, "I am so grateful to God for what has happened to my husband. Now the children and I have what we need to eat and wear and we have all the comforts of a good home." So you can see that Christianity pays off financially in the home.

2. *Christianity pays off financially in business.* The man who applies the principles of Jesus in his business will have the help that the Lord has promised him. Mr. J. L. Kraft drove his horse, Paddy, from door-to-door, trying to sell cheese. But he soon failed. Then, upon his knees, he promised to take the Lord into partnership with him. He became a more active Christian and his business became prosperous. Now the Kraft Cheese Company has become a tremendous enterprise, because a man decided to go into partnership with Jesus.

In Cincinnati Mr. A. Nash ran a clothing business which he tried to conduct according to Christian principles. He was called "Golden Rule Nash." He became rich, gave God His part, and before he died he gave his firm to his employees. Jesus said, "But seek ye first the kingdom of God, and his righteousness; and all these things shall be added unto you" (Matthew 6:33). And He was talking about material things. It would pay every Christian business man to put Jesus first.

3. *Christianity would pay off financially in government.* The larger part of our national budget goes for defense purposes. If it were not for sin, if all nations practiced Christianity, this would not be necessary.

Then think of all the money we spend on courts and officers and jails and penitentiaries. If all citizens were good Christians, we would not need these things. Just take one case. When a crime is committed, we must have some men employed to arrest the criminal. Then the state must give the man board and lodging, it must pay the expenses of the court and attorneys and judges and a jury. Then the man must be provided with board and lodging and clothing for the period of his prison term. No wonder our taxes are so high. But if all citizens were good Christians there would be no crime and the government would profit financially, leaving money to be spent for the benefit of mankind.

III. It Pays to Be a Christian From an Intellectual Standpoint

I realize that many infidels are brilliant along certain lines and many criminals are above average in intelligence. But as a whole criminals are of a lower mental ability. Shelley said, "Christianity dwarfs the mind." How wrong he was — it is sin that dwarfs and dulls the mind. The greatest poets and writers, the greatest artists, the greatest statesmen and rulers have been Christians.

The Psalmist said, "The fear of the LORD is the beginning of wisdom . . ." (Psalm 111:10). If you know all the things in all the books and all the schools and know not Christ, you don't have true wisdom. It was the fool who said in his heart, "There is no God" (Psalms 14:1; 53:1).

IV. IT PAYS TO BE A CHRISTIAN FROM AN ETERNAL STANDPOINT

There's heaven to be gained and a hell to be shunned. But even if there is no hereafter, if the grave is the end of it all, it is profitable to follow Christ right here and now. The happiest people are not those who are chasing sin. Oh, they think they are happy, their hollow laugh rings out at night, but the next day their head is aching and they say, "What an awful party that was last night."

But the worldling, the sinner, is miserable compared to the Christian. The happiest and most useful people are those who are living for Christ and righteousness and goodness.

Yes, it pays to be a Christian here, but we'll never realize the full value of what it means to follow Christ until we reach heaven. Then we'll come to know just what we've been saved from and what we've been saved to. We'll know the horrors of hell and the blessings of heaven. Then we'll thank God throughout eternity that we gave our hearts and lives to the Lord Jesus.

1. *It pays to be a Christian when you come to life's last hour.* A preacher was called to the bedside of a forty-four-year-old man who lay dying. The man said, "I want to thank you for persuading me to make a big investment in the religion of Christ. It was the best thing I ever did."

When you come down to the end of the way, when you realize that you have just a little time left, when you look back over your life, what will be the thing that mattered most? It will not be money or friends or fame. You'll forget everything else and rejoice that you came to Christ. In your dying hour you'll see how it paid to be a Christian.

2. *It pays out yonder in God's great eternity.* Throughout eternity the lost man in hell will gnash his teeth and cry out, "Oh, if I only had, if I only had obeyed God's voice and given my heart to Jesus." But throughout eternity the saved man will rejoice in heaven and sing, "Oh, happy day that fixed my choice on Christ my Saviour and my God."

When you meet your loved ones in glory you'll say, "I have been longing to see you all of these years. Now I see how my Christianity paid off." When you find sweet rest after a weary life, you'll say, "Oh, it paid off." When all your dreams come true, you'll say, "Yes, it paid to be a Christian."

Then when you see Jesus face to face, when you feel the love of His great heart and the tenderness of His look, surely you'll say, "Yes, Lord, I see now that it really paid to be a Christian."

5.

Jesus Is All You Need
John 6:66-69

Paul one day looked out upon life. He thought of all the problems of an individual, he thought of all the troubles men had and all the burdens they had to carry. And he said, ". . . who is sufficient for these things?" (II Corinthians 2:16). There is only one answer to this question. No human being, however great, can meet every need of life. But there is One who can. His name is Jesus. He is the adequate, the all-sufficient Saviour. He meets every need of life. In Him and with His help we can face up to life and all of its problems.

Our text comes just after Christ had fed the five thousand. He had proved that He could meet man's physical needs. Now the crowds began to gather around Him. They cared nothing for Him, but just for what He could do for them. They were not interested in Him as a Saviour, they simply wanted to be fed, they wanted something for nothing. So Jesus preached a sermon to them, a sermon in which He appealed for them to surrender their lives, a sermon in which He demanded that they give instead of receive.

They were willing to follow Him as long as He was feeding them and requiring nothing of them. But when He began to tell them what would be expected of them if they continued to follow Him, the great crowd turned away and went back to the world. It's the same way today. Let a man preach the free grace of God, let him tell of all a man receives as a Christian, let him tell of the "pie in the sky, bye and bye," and men will follow him and call him a great preacher. But let him call upon people to forsake the world and follow Jesus, let him ask for money for the work of the Lord, let him ask them to go out into the highways and hedges to witness for Christ, and the majority will turn their backs upon Him.

In the early days of my ministry I went to be the pastor of a

37

church in a small town. We were having good congregations
and fine services. One of the men of the church was especially
enthusiastic about the young new preacher and his messages.
He made it a point to invite others to hear his new pastor.
Then I preached two sermons on the stewardship of life and
money. And that man lost his enthusiasm and stopped coming
to church. It is so easy for some people to say "Amen" when
the preacher speaks about what Christ gives us, but they are
strangely silent when he speaks of what we should give Christ.

As the crowds began to leave Jesus He sadly turned to His
disciples and said, "Will ye also go away?" And bold, brave
Peter, who often said the wrong thing, said the right thing this
time. "Lord," he said, "to whom shall we go? thou hast the
words of eternal life. And we believe and are sure that thou art
that Christ, the Son of the living God" (John 6:68, 69).

There are many different kinds of people in the world, the
rich and the poor, the young and the old, the ignorant and the
educated. But fundamentally they all have the same three basic
needs. They need forgiveness for the past, strength and guidance
for the present, and hope for the future.

I. WE NEED FORGIVENESS FOR THE PAST

As we look over our past we see one sin after another along
the way. If nothing is done about our sin, we shall be forever
banished from the presence of God and plunged into an eternal
hell. Sin is like a great rock tied around the neck, pulling us
down into the waters. Only Christ can cut that rope, only He
can rescue us. Sin is like a cloud between us and God. Only
Christ can melt that cloud and enable us to see the face of God.

Jesus was in Capernaum, preaching in a certain house. Four
men went out and brought a sick man and placed him before
the Master. Jesus said to the sick man, ". . . thy sins be forgiven thee" (Mark 2:5). The crowd began to murmur and
someone said, "That's blasphemy, only God can do that, only God
can forgive sin." But Jesus was God in the flesh and this power
was vested in Him. To prove that He was God He healed the
man and sent him on his way. The church can't forgive sin,
the priest can't forgive sin, the preacher can't forgive sin. Only
God can do that and Christ is God.

John tells us that ". . . the blood of Jesus Christ his Son

cleanseth us from all sin" (I John 1:7). And because of that cleansing, that forgiveness, we are restored to favor with God and given a home in heaven.

At Pearl Harbor a sailor manned an anti-aircraft battery on a battleship. He fought for four hours and was finally taken to the hospital with burns and shrapnel wounds. He received eight transfusions of blood from the Red Cross bloodbank, and this saved his life. When he recovered he said, "I am going back to America and give back pint by pint all the blood that was needed to save me, and more besides." Listen, it was Jesus' blood that saved us from sin. We can't pay Him back, we'll never be able to do that. But we ought, in gratitude, to serve Him with the best that we have.

> But drops of grief can ne'er repay
> The debt of love I owe;
> Here Lord I give myself away,
> 'Tis all that I can do.
> — *Isaac Watts*

Yes, Jesus is sufficient, He forgives all our sins of the past and brings us into right relationship to God.

II. WE NEED STRENGTH AND GUIDANCE FOR THE PRESENT

Some people go to fortune-tellers for guidance, some write to newspaper columnists, some consult their friends. Now we are all human and no human being can give us perfect guidance. No one knows what tomorrow may bring, no one can look into the future. But the Bible tells us where to seek guidance. *James 1:5* says, "If any of you lack wisdom, let him ask of God, that giveth to all men liberally, and upbraideth not; and it shall be given him."

Jesus knows our past, our present, our future. There is no uncertainty in Him. Nothing will ever come up in our lives that is not known to Him. He sees the end from the beginning. And because He knows all about us He can help us.

Before a person is converted he has temptations on every side, together with sorrows, tears and heartaches. After his conversion he has these same things, but there is a difference. Before his conversion he is alone as he faces these things; after his conversion he has Someone to help him, even Jesus. Hyman Appelman, the evangelist, said that just after he was converted he had many temptations and troubles, but they would last only until he could get to his prayer closet and no longer. Why don't we run to Jesus with everything?

A boy in the air corps was afraid that he would "wash out" and fail to get his wings. One day the instructor said, "This is your last chance." As the boy started up on his flight he was quite nervous. But being a Christian he reached up to God in prayer. Suddenly the 23rd Psalm came to his mind, "The Lord is my shepherd." He repeated the entire psalm to himself, his nerves were soon calm and his flight was perfect. He passed the test and received his wings. Whatever your need is today, Jesus is ready to supply it.

A certain family lost three children from diptheria. On Easter Sunday the father and mother and their remaining child went to Sunday school and church. The father presided over his department, and read the Bible lesson, the mother taught her class. Then they sat quietly in the church and listened to the pastor's sermon. People said, "How can they do it?" A 15-year-old girl said to her father, "They really believe it, don't they?" "Believe what?" he asked. She answered, "The whole big thing, the resurrection and all." "Of course," said her father, "all Christians believe it." "But not that way," said the wise teen-ager.

We need to believe it all, not just as mental assent, but with the whole heart. Jesus is alive, He is real, He can help us when life's problems become too complex and life's burdens too heavy.

III. WE NEED HOPE FOR THE FUTURE

If our Lord tarries we shall all go through the experience of death. You can stay away from church, you can fail to read the Bible, you can say "no" to the Holy Spirit, you can reject Christ's offer of free salvation. But there is one officer of God that you cannot put off, the Angel of Death. When God sends him to write "the end" to life, you cannot push him away. You can't say, "Come back some other day." You are powerless against him. ". . . it is appointed unto men once to die, but after this the judgment" (Hebrews 9:27).

But when the doctors and the nurses cannot help you, you can have One by your side who will help you. He has said that He will never leave you nor forsake you, even when you walk down through the valley of the shadow of death. He is the king and conqueror of death, so there is no fear for the Christian with Jesus by his side.

Then someday the Christian faces the judgment seat of Christ. There'll be no fear for him there, condemnation will have passed. It will be a time of blessing and reward. Not a single Christian will ever appear before the Great White Throne judgment. Only the lost will be there.

The Christian may have little of this world's goods. But he is rich in hope and that hope is free for the asking. Jesus says, "Put your trust in Me. I will forgive the past, I will help you through the present, I will give you hope for the future."

A chaplain in France tells of three pictures that a soldier showed him. The first picture showed a man with the ruins of a city all around him. And the inscription read, "The past has deceived me." The second picture showed a serpent trying to climb a slick pole, an impossible task. And the inscription read, "The present overmasters me." The third picture showed a cannon, with a man looking down into it. And that inscription read, "The future appalls me."

That's the way it is if you don't know Christ. The past deceives you, the present overmasters you, the future appalls you. But if you have Jesus the past is covered by the blood, you have a very present help for every day, and you have a bright prospect for the future.

Thank God, Jesus Christ is sufficient. He is all you need.

good

6.

The Greatest Fact of History

I Corinthians 15:12-26

There are two great facts about Christianity which make it different from all other religions of the world. First, Christianity is vitally bound up with a Person. That Person is the Lord Jesus Christ, God's only begotten Son. He was born of a virgin, He lived a sinless life, He performed many mighty miracles, He died a vicarious death on a shameful cross, He was buried in a borrowed tomb, He rose from the dead and ascended into heaven, from whence He will return some day to set up His everlasting kingdom.

Yes, Christianity centers around the person of the Lord Jesus Christ. You can be a good Buddhist and know little or nothing of Buddha. You can be a good Mohammedan and know nothing of Mohammed. These religions are religions of form and ritual. But you can't be a Christian without knowing Christ. You can't be a Christian without trusting, loving and following the Lord Jesus. Christianity is Christ.

We become Christians not by accepting a creed or a system of ethics, but by receiving a Person, the Lord Jesus. "But as many as received him, to them gave he power to become the sons of God, even to them that believe on his name" (John 1:12). Jesus says, "Behold, I stand at the door, and knock: if any man hear my voice, and open the door, I will come in to him, and will sup with him, and he with me" (Revelation 3:20).

The second fact of Christianity which makes it different from every other world religion is that its Founder is alive. Although Christianity was founded 2,000 years ago, its Founder still lives. No other religion can make that boast. You can go to Mecca and the Mohammedan will say, "Here is the grave of our founder Mohammed." But when you go to the grave where Jesus was buried in Jerusalem, you hear the angel from heaven saying, "He is not here, for he is risen . . ." (Matthew 28:6).

The cross is the symbol of the Christian religion, but it is an empty cross and not a crucifix. He is alive, our Leader — our Founder is alive forevermore. He is the very center of our religion, a living Lord, a Saviour who saves and keeps, who walks and talks with His people.

I. His Resurrection Is the World's Greatest Fact

It is the greatest fact phenomenally. Nothing more phenomenal ever happened in this world. It was the miracle of all miracles. Can you imagine how greatly you would be impressed if one you had known and whose funeral you had attended, should rise and come to visit you three days after the funeral?

The resurrection of Jesus Christ means more to the human race than anything that has ever happened. The Bible teaches us that it is the most significant event in the world's history. Let us see what Paul says about it.

He says that if Christ is not risen, we preachers are false witnesses. Think of all the great and small preachers of all the centuries. Think of all the millions who have been converted under these preachers. Well, if Christ did not rise from the dead, all this preaching has been a worthless thing and a waste of time and energy. But Christ did rise from the dead and the preaching of His Gospel has been a mighty factor in the life of the world.

Paul then says that if Christ is not risen, our faith is vain and we are still in our sin. Think of it, our sins still stand between us and God, our faith is of no value, we are forever lost.

He goes on to say that if Christ is not risen, our loved ones are gone forever. This means that they have perished, we'll never see them again. You can see, therefore, that our whole religious system, our salvation, our faith, our preaching, our works, our giving, all are in vain if Jesus is still dead. But Paul says this is not the case. He says, "But now is Christ risen from the dead, and become the firstfruits of them that slept" (I Corinthians 15:20).

II. His Resurrection Is a Thoroughly Authenticated Fact

If anyone will take the Bible and examine all the evidence, then look at the effect that belief in the resurrection had upon

His followers, they must certainly know that Jesus rose from the dead.

In other days an Infidel's Club existed in London. Two of the club's most prominent members were appointed to disprove two things, the resurrection of Christ, and the conversion of Paul. At a given time these two men returned to make their report. The first one said, "I have carefully examined all the evidence and I am convinced that Christ did rise from the dead. I have accepted Him as my Saviour and from henceforth I shall be His disciple." The second man said, "I also have carefully examined the evidence and I am convinced that Paul was genuinely converted and that he was changed from a murderer to a minister. I, too, have accepted Paul's Saviour as my Saviour."

Yes, if any man will come to the Bible and examine all the evidence with an open mind, the Holy Spirit will lead him into the truth of the resurrection.

III. His Resurrection Proved His Deity

Jesus Christ made claims that only a God could make. He said, ". . . he that hath seen me hath seen the Father. . ." (John 14:9). He said, "I and my Father are one" (John 10:30). He said, ". . . no man cometh unto the Father, but by me" (John 14:6). He said, "I am the resurrection and the life: he that believeth in me, though he were dead, yet shall he live" (John 11:25). He said, ". . . every one which seeth the Son, and believeth on him, may have everlasting life: and I will raise him up at the last day" (John 6:40).

Look at the claims that Christ made here. He claimed to be God. He claimed to be able to give everlasting life. He claimed to be able to raise men up at the last day. In order to be able to make such claims He had to be more than a mere man. And we know He is more than a mere man when we see Him rise up from the grave. And God put His seal of approval upon every claim that Jesus made.

Suppose that I said to you, "I can jump over a 5-foot fence." You might not believe me. But suppose one day you saw me do the superhuman thing of jumping over a 25-foot fence. You would surely know then that I could jump a 5-foot fence. Jesus claimed to be able to do many things which seemed impossible. But when we see Him doing the unbelievable, unheard-of thing of rising from the dead, we know that He can do anything.

IV. HIS RESURRECTION GUARANTEES OUR JUSTIFICATION

In J. Wilbur Chapman's great song, "One Day," he says that "rising He justified freely forever." Now what do we mean by "justification"? It is God's process which causes us to appear before Him as if we had never sinned. This comes only when our sins are covered by the blood of Christ and this comes about through our faith in the risen Saviour.

In Romans 5 and 8 we are told that we are justified by Him who rose from the dead and who sits at the right hand of God. In *Romans 4:5* we read, "But to him that worketh not, but believeth on him that justifieth the ungodly, his faith is counted for righteousness."

A poor lost sinner comes to Christ and the great miracle happens. God justifies him and makes him in His sight as if he had never sinned. And this can come about only through faith in the risen Christ.

A young man was in one of our state penitentiaries, serving a sentence for forgery. Through the influence of friends he received a pardon from the governor. The prison chaplain called the young man into his office and said to him, "You ought to be very happy." "No," answered the young man, "I am miserable." "Don't you appreciate what the governor and your friends have done for you?" asked the chaplain. "Yes, sir," said the young man, "but there is something the governor cannot do. I have a pardon but I am still guilty. I am ashamed to face my friends and my mother." The governor could give him a pardon, but he couldn't take away the guilt, he couldn't make him as if he had never sinned. But God is greater than any governor. He not only pardons but He justifies. Then when at last we stand before Him, we shall stand without shame.

V. HIS RESURRECTION PROVES THAT WE SHALL ALSO RISE

Job asked the question, "If a man die, shall he live again?" (Job 14:14). And Paul answers by saying that Christ rose from the dead and is become the first-fruits of them that slept. When you see one apple on a tree you know that others are to follow.

So Jesus arose as the first fruit of the resurrection and we shall follow Him.

The Christians in Thessalonica were disturbed because some of their loved ones had died. They were concerned lest their deceased friends and relatives would miss the joy of meeting Jesus when He returned to earth. Paul told them that they were not to sorrow "even as others which have no hope" (I Thessalonians 4:13). There is no hope for those who don't know the Lord as Saviour. He explained to them that when Jesus returned God would bring with Him all those who had died in Christ. He brought Jesus from the tomb and He will bring us from our tombs.

He goes on to say that "the Lord himself shall descend from heaven with a shout . . ." (I Thessalonians 4:16). Then he tells us that the dead in Christ will arise first. There it is, there is the guarantee of our resurrection.

We'll have a new body then. A dear old preacher said to his wife, "I can hardly get up the hill now. There was a time when I could run up." Then he said, "When I am 33 I'll be all right." "What do you mean?" asked his wife, "you are more than twice 33 now." He answered, "When my body is raised it will be like Jesus' body and He was a perfect man at 33." The preacher was right. We sing about "the land where we'll never grow old." Moses had been gone 1500 years, Elijah had been gone 750, when they came back on the Mount of Transfiguration, but they had not grown old. The best is yet to be for the Christian. Someday He'll take us up to be with Him, hallelujah!

VI. His Resurrection Is a Picture of the Rapture

The rapture will be that time I have just spoken of when Christ shall come and raise up all Christians, those who are dead and those who are alive, to be with Him forever. Paul said we would be caught up "together with them." With whom? With our loved ones and all the saints of God. "For now we see through a glass, darkly; but then face to face: now I know in part; but then shall I know even as also I am known" (I Corinthians 13:12).

Often we hear someone who is enjoying this world say, "This is the life." No, this is death down here. We die a little every day, our bodies are decaying, we are growing older, we suffer the aches and pains of a dying body. But that's the life, when one day Jesus takes us up to live with Him. Because He lives we also shall live.

An evangelist was conducting meetings in Southern California. A rich man wanted to be nice to him, so he put the preacher in one of the finest and most beautiful hotels on the coast. The hotel had a marvelous view and every morning the preacher would go out on the balcony of his room and enjoy the view. One morning a boy came in to straighten up the hotel room. The preacher said, "Isn't this a glorious view?" "Yes, sir, it is." answered the boy. Then the preacher said, "I think this is the nicest place in America, don't you?" "No, sir, I don't," the boy replied. "Do you know of a better place?" the preacher asked. "Yes, sir," the boy said, "it's nicer than this back in Arkansas." "Son," said the preacher, "would you compare Arkansas with Southern California?" And the boy replied, "California may suit some people better, but Arkansas suits me better." "Why is that?" asked the preacher. And the boy answered, "Because all of my folks are back there."

We are going to be caught up with our folks. Heaven isn't just the pearly gates, the golden streets, the many mansions, it is people. Our people are going up one day. Then all of their faults will be gone and all of our imperfections will be gone. We will be with them and with Jesus forever.

I'm so glad that Jesus rose from the dead. In doing so He made our salvation possible. I'm glad that we can follow Him in this world and go up someday to be forever with Him and all those we have loved. So I say as I think of the resurrection and all it means, "Hallelujah, what a Saviour!"

7.

Peace in the Valley

Psalm 46:1 and Psalm 23

A man on a mountaintop realizes that he cannot stay there forever. The view is magnificent, the air is fresh and pure. But he knows the time is coming when he must go back down into the valley, where the air is often thick and the view unpleasant. Likewise the Christian realizes that he cannot always rest upon the mountaintop of life. Peace and joy and happiness are his on the mountaintop, but because he knows life he knows he must often go down into the valley of sorrow and trouble and even death at the end of the way.

But here's the wondrous thing about Christianity. Your serenity and happiness may be broken by the troubles of life, but you can still find peace in the valley if Jesus is there with you. And has He not promised to be there? Is not Christ in the valley as well as on the mountaintop? He has said, ". . . lo, I am with you alway, even unto the end of the world" (Matthew 28:20). He has said, "I will never leave thee nor forsake thee" (Hebrews 13:5). David said, "Yea, though I walk through the valley of the shadow of death, I will fear no evil . . . (Psalm 23:4).

When World War II first involved America, after the attack on Pearl Harbor, President Roosevelt said, "The American people must prepare for dark days ahead. The casualty lists will grow and sorrow will come to many homes." We saw that happen. Many of our families received those telegrams from the Adjutant General, giving them the sad news that a loved one had lost his life in battle. And then we saw how they were sustained and comforted by the grace of God.

Every person needs to get ready for that valley experience. The car containing your loved ones begins a journey of a thousand miles. Remember that hundreds of people are killed on the highways and it could happen to them. The plane takes off from the airport but it may come down in flames. Your loved

48

ones lie down to sleep but they may not arise. They go to work but they may not return. Are you ready for the unseen tragedy that lurks around every corner? Do you have a Comforter like Jesus?

A young couple met in my church, fell in love and were married. He was a big, strong fellow who had made a good record in the navy. They moved to another city and some years later I went to that city to conduct a revival. One night I had dinner with this young couple. We had an enjoyable time of fellowship as he related some of his submarine experiences. The next night he was driving to another city to hear another preacher friend and was involved in a tragic automobile accident. They brought him back to our city and I visited him often in the hospital. He was completely paralyzed from the neck down and he could not speak. The doctors said he would be an invalid for the rest of his life.

Oh, we need something in our hearts to prepare us for these valley experiences. Some years ago I was riding on a fine train. The sunlight splashed in the windows and lighted up the entire car. Then the porter came through and began to turn on the lights in the pullman car. I wondered why he would turn on the lights when the sun was shining brightly into the car. But soon I understood. The train plunged into a long, dark tunnel. If the porter had not turned on the lights we would have been in total darkness.

So we go along in the sunlight of life, happy and gay. Then suddenly we are plunged into the darkness of sorrow and tragedy and heartbreak. We need a light before we go into that tunnel, before we enter into that darkness. And that Light we need is Jesus, the Light of the world.

Job went down into the dark valley. He lost his children, his property, his health. But he had something to sustain him. He said, "Though he slay me, yet will I trust in him . . ." (Job 13: 15). And he said, "I know that my redeemer liveth . . ." (Job 19:25). He blindly trusted God and God rewarded his faith. Later he was better off in every way than ever before.

Paul went down into that dark valley. After his conversion to Christ he lost friends, position, everything. He suffered all sorts of indignities for Christ's sake. In one place he gives an account of the tribulations and troubles which he had endured. But he rejoiced in the Lord and said, "And we know that all things work together for good to them that love God, to them who are the called according to his purpose" (Romans 8:28). He said that the things that were formed against him had turned out for his benefit. In the dark valley he had walked with Jesus and it had been a profitable walk.

John went down into that valley. He was banished to the Isle of Patmos, separated from home and friends and loved ones. But God lifted the curtain of eternity and let the light shine upon him. He saw heaven and all its glories. And he saw Jesus waiting for him. No wonder he cried out, "Even so, come, Lord Jesus" (Revelation 22:20).

Yes, the dark valleys await us all. But those who have had a mountaintop experience at Calvary have Christ with them in the valley.

I. God's People Have Never Had It Easy

Once they were in slavery in the land of Egypt. Their lives were hard and bitter, so they cried out to God for help. And God heard their cry. He overcame their enemies and sent Moses to lead them toward the Promised Land. When they came to the Red Sea they were hemmed in on every side. The sea was in front of them, the mountains were on either side and Pharaoh's army was behind them, bent on taking them back into bondage. Pharaoh said, "I'll get them." But God said, "I'll deliver my people." And He did. He destroyed Pharaoh and his army and brought His people out.

When Hezekiah was King, Sennacherib came against him with a mighty army. He sent an insulting, blasphemous letter to the king. "I know you trust in God," he wrote, "but we have no fear. We have conquered other nations that trusted in their gods and we'll conquer and destroy you." When Hezekiah received the letter, he did not go into a panic. He did not call in his generals for a conference of war nor did he prepare a surrender message. He went to church and spread the letter before the Lord, so that God could read it over his shoulder. "Lord," he prayed, "You see our plight. But all of our faith is in You, we turn it all over to You. Come to the rescue of Your people." God heard that prayer. That night His angel came down and slew 185,000 of Sennacherib's army and Hezekiah's country was saved. Yes, God cares for His people.

One dark day His enemies slew Jesus on Calvary's cross. They exulted over their victory. "We have Him now," they said. "He'll bother us no more. His cause will soon die out." But God said, "His hour has just begun." And God raised Him up and caused Him to become the mightiest Power who ever touched this world.

There came a time when the Christian religion seemed to be dying. It was being almost killed by formalism and ritualism. But God raised up Martin Luther who quoted God's Word, ". . . The just shall live by faith" (Galatians 3:11) and led the Christian world back to God and salvation by faith. Christianity flourished again in the period called the Reformation.

When George Washington camped at Valley Forge it was a dark hour for the fledgling nation. His armies were ill-clad, poorly armed and half-starved. Defeat was staring them in the face. But George Washington was a man of prayer. He not only believed in the American cause for which he was fighting, he also believed in God. So he knelt in the snow and pled for God's help. God heard his prayer and gave him the victory, and made of America the greatest nation under the sun.

On December 7th, 1941, the Japanese attacked Pearl Harbor. Wave after wave of bombers swept over the harbor, crippling our ships, killing our men and practically wiping out our fleet. If the Japanese had returned the next day they could have taken over Hawaii, then they could have moved in on our West Coast and captured our country. Why didn't the Japanese come back? There is no military answer to the question. The only answer is a spiritual one. God took a hand in the matter and saved America!

And as God works in history, so He works in individual lives. His people go down into the valley where everything seems dark, but He brings them out into the sunlight.

II. GOD GIVES GRACE TO BEAR ALL THAT COMES OUR WAY

God said a fine word to Paul, "I know you have troubles," He said. "I know about your thorn in the flesh, but my grace is sufficient for thee." God is certainly a God of sufficiency. He made not one star, but millions. He made not one tree or flower, but He covered the earth with them. He piled up not one mountain, but He scattered them all over the world. And

His grace and strength and power are sufficient to help every man in the world.

God's grace is sufficient to save us. It is sufficient to forgive us when we have sinned. God's grace is sufficient in the hour of trial and suffering. It is sufficient in the hour of sorrow. God's grace is sufficient in the hour of death.

When I was attending seminary I preached every other Sunday in a small North Texas town. I often spent the night in the home of a couple who had lost their only son many years before that time in World War I. On several occasions this couple would point to the picture of that boy and tell me how much they missed him. But they were faithful to God and their church. They went about their duties, and God comforted them.

Elisha was in trouble on one occasion. The king sent an army out to capture him and this meant his death. Elisha's servant saw the army coming and was sore afraid. "Master, what are we going to do?" he asked Elisha. "They will surely put us both to death." But Elisha laughed and said, "Son, you see just these human forces. I see something else. I am going to ask God to open your eyes." And Elisha prayed, "Lord, open the young man's eyes and show him what You have out there." And God did open the servant's eyes and he looked up and saw the mountains filled with the hosts of God. He knew that Elisha's enemies didn't have a chance. Oh, if God be for us, who can be against us? Sometimes the whole world seems to be against us, but God is bigger than all of our enemies and He will deliver us.

So when trouble comes don't go to pieces, go to God. Remember *Romans 8:28*. I have seen how this truth works scores of times. Something happened to me that hurt me. It certainly wasn't something good. But later on I would look back and see that this thing, coupled with other things, was working out to bless me, and I said, "Thank You, Lord." He knows how to deliver His people out of all their trouble.

When I was a boy I enjoyed reading. Often I would take a book to bed and read it there. My father knew that I ought to be asleep. He would see the light shining from under the door and he would call out, "Herschel, put out that light and go to sleep." But I would be at the most interesting part of the story. The heroine would be in the clutches of the villain and the hero would be in serious trouble and I would be concerned about them. But I would say, "All right, papa." Then I would turn over quickly to the last page of my book. There I would learn that the villain had been defeated and the hero and heroine were living happily ever afterwards. Then I would close the book, turn out the light and lie awake thinking of the story. I would say, "Old Villain, in the middle of the book you think you are somebody, you have my friends in your power. But if you just knew what's coming to you, you wouldn't be so sure of yourself."

Now we look at the world today. It seems that Satan has the upper hand, he is ruling nations and causing trouble everywhere. He is giving God's people a hard time. But I have looked over into the back of the Book, God's Book. I know what's going to happen. The old devil is going to be bound and cast into the lake of fire. Then all of our troubles will be over and God's people will be reigning with Jesus!

So we can say, "Satan, you're running things now but someday things are going to be different. God's children aren't always going to be wrapped in sorrow and trouble. All will be well then for we'll be at home where you can never touch or tempt us."

Yes, there may be some dark days ahead for you and me. There's only one way for us to prepare for those days. We must fill our hearts with Christ and His promises. Then when trouble comes we'll find peace in the valley.

8.

Tremendous Needs for Troublous Times
Matthew 6:31-34

The Bible uses many small words of one syllable, words which are full of great meaning. There is the word "lost." Just think of what that will mean throughout eternity, separated from God and loved ones and all things good. Then there is the word "so." "God so loved the world." No one can measure how much that little word means. God loves us in the superlative degree, beyond all other loves in heaven and earth. Then there is the word "kept." This means that once we are His we are His forever. He keeps us as the apple of His eye. Then there is the word "go." We are to go into all the world, telling men about the saving grace of Christ.

In this message we look at another little word, the word "need." We need health, money, food, clothing, an education. Well, Jesus talked about our needs for He is interested in every phase of our being. He tells us that the Heavenly Father knows about our needs, then He tells us how to get everything we need. "But seek ye first the kingdom of God, and his righteousness; and all these things shall be added unto you" (Matthew 6:33).

Now let us think of our spiritual needs in the light of the day in which we are living.

I. WE NEED CONFIDENCE

1. *We need confidence in God.* Jesus tells us to "have faith in God." If we had a greater faith, we would not fret and worry as we do. I go down to the bank to borrow some money. I sign a note and receive the money. Why? Because the banker has confidence in my promise to pay. Well, God has made some promises. Don't we have confidence in Him? Surely God will keep His promises.

The loan at the bank is based on certain conditions. So are the promises of God. He tells us that we must do something first. We must seek first the kingdom of God and His righteousness. We must put Him first in all things. Then He says that He will add unto us those things that we need.

Do you have confidence in God? He says that He cares for you, that He will supply all your needs. Do we believe that? No, we worry, we fret, we push our own plans, we run ahead of God. Yet He says that a sparrow doesn't fall to the ground without His notice. He numbers the hairs of our heads. Will such a God let you fall? Paul says, "But my God shall supply all your need according to his riches in glory by Christ Jesus" (Philippians 4:19). That's the kind of a God He is. Don't you have confidence in Him?

A storm arose at sea and a certain man on a ship was frightened and worried. Then a Bible text leaped into his mind. "Behold, he that keepeth Israel shall neither slumber nor sleep" (Psalm 121:4). He said to himself, "There is no need for both of us to stay awake. I will go to sleep and leave the storm in His hands.". And that's what He wants us to do in all the storms of life.

2. *We need confidence in ourselves.* No man ever did a thing until he felt in his heart that he could do it. And what is the Christian basis for confidence in ourselves? It is found in *Philippians 4:13,* "I can do all things through Christ which strengtheneth me."

When the great missionary, Robert Morrison, was leaving for China, someone said to him, "Do you expect to make any impression on that great Chinese Empire?" And he answered, "No, but I expect God will." And God did, using the talents of that dedicated man.

3. *We need confidence in others.* Yes, there are many crooked, hypocritical people. On the other hand there are many good people, there are many sincere Christians. Jesus saw the hypocrites and called them "whited sepulchres." But He saw the good that was in Simon Peter and Saul of Tarsus and John Mark. And their service to God fully justified His faith. It is easy for us to find flaws in people, because they are so much like ourselves, but we need to have faith in people. Some of them will disap-

point us, it is true, but some of them will gloriously reward our confidence in them.

II. WE NEED CONTENTMENT

Paul suffered many things for Christ, but he said, ". . . I have learned, in whatsoever state I am, therewith to be content" (Philippians 4:11). Again he said in *I Timothy 6:6*, "But godliness with contentment is great gain." Really and truly, no man has contentment without godliness.

1. *We owe it to God to be contented.* If a father gives his son everything and the son still grumbles, that hurts the father. Yet God gives us everything and we go on grumbling, wounding God, dishonoring Him. But "why should the children of a King go mourning all their days?"

Now there is a difference in being contented and being satisfied. We are always to be contented, putting all of our faith in God, but we are never to be satisfied. We must keep pressing on, trying always to live a better life and to give God a nobler service.

Someone asked a great artist, "Which is your masterpiece?" And he answered, "My next picture." We are to keep striving, keeping our minds centered on Christ. "Thou wilt keep him in perfect peace, whose mind is stayed on thee" (Isaiah 26:3).

2. *We owe it to ourselves to be contented.* We'll be happier, we'll live longer, we'll serve God better if we practice the art of contentment.

3. *We owe it to others to be contented.* Jesus said, "Ye are the light of the world . . ." (Matthew 5:14). But how can you shine for Him if you are not contented? Suppose that a man were lost in a swamp and that you wanted to help him find the way out. You would stand in a high place and wave a bright light for him to see. But if you carelessly let the light go out that would not be fair to the man. Well, men are in the darkness of discouragement, despair and sin. When we let the light of our Christian contentment shine, it will give them hope. If our Christianity is the grumbling, fretful kind, it won't be the kind our neighbor will want.

III. We Need Co-operation

Here is a man who wants a church for himself and his family. He wants them to hear the Gospel, he wants them to enjoy good music, he wants them to study the Bible and have all the advantages of a good church. But he can afford to give only a few dollars per week. So what is he to do? He cooperates with other Christians and then together they build a church for themselves and their families.

Another man feels it his duty to help carry out the spirit of the Great Commission. He cannot go "into all the world" to carry the Gospel and he is not able to support a missionary alone. So he cooperates with others, they pool their resources and missionaries are sent to the ends of the earth. In this manner all of our world-wide work is carried on.

Go into a great factory and listen to the hum of the machinery there. There may be a thousand different types and pieces of machinery there, yet they all are working together, each piece fitting in and working smoothly with every other piece. And the result is power. And out of power comes a product. If one piece of machinery gets out of line, the whole process fails. So in the church there are many members. Their talents are varied and different. One member can do one thing well and another member can do another thing well. Now if they all cooperate, if they all work together smoothly for the glory of God, the power will come and God's work will be done.

Paul said "we are labourers together with God . . ." (I Corinthians 4:9). Here is a wonderful picture, with you on one side of the load and God on the other. He is carrying the heaviest part but you will get the greatest joy out of it.

IV. We Need Courage

When Paul journeyed to Rome he walked up the famous Appian Way and we read that ". . . he thanked God, and took courage" (Acts 28:15). He thanked God for bringing him through a terrible storm and a destructive shipwreck. And he received fresh courage as he remembered the goodness of God. We, too, should find new courage as we remember that Christ will never leave us nor forsake us.

Hugh Walpole said, " 'Tisn't life that matters, it's the courage ye bring to it." And another said, "The chief thing in life is a stiff backbone."

1. *We need courage to stand up for our convictions.* Such a course may make us unpopular, but we must stand up for our Christian convictions even if the skies fall. When President Hayes was in office a young reporter attended a banquet given in the president's honor. This reporter was a total abstainer. When he asked the president for a copy of his speech, the president asked him why he did not drink the liquor served at the banquet. The reporter replied, "Because I wanted to get the facts straight for my paper." The president was so pleased that he gave him a copy of his speech and a friendship was formed between them that lasted for years. Who was the young reporter? He was Edward W. Bok, who later served as editor of the *Ladies Home Journal.* The famous Bok tower in Florida is a memorial to him. A man with such convictions is bound to go up.

2. *We need courage to bear bravely the sorrows of life.* "Into each life some rain must fall." But God does not forsake us in such hours. ". . . as thy days, so shall thy strength be" (Deuteronomy 33:25). He measures the strength to the demand. We must not say of life, "I cannot stand it," but rather, "With God's help, I will bear that which comes upon me."

3. *We need courage to make the necessary sacrifices cheerfully.* Sir Wilfred Grenfell worked for 40 years as a missionary and doctor in the frozen areas of Labrador. When someone spoke to him about the sacrifices he had made, he replied, "I know nothing about any sacrifices."

We will never be called upon to make the sacrifices that some have made, but some Christians think they are making a sacrifice when they come to church on Sunday night or Wednesday night.

Isn't it sad that a Christian for whom Christ gladly died has to sacrifice seeing some television program on Sunday night! How in the world does he stand it? And then that Christian spends hundreds of dollars on sports and trips and pleasures, and must give a dollar per week to his church! It's enough to break an angel's heart. Why don't we quit "kidding" ourselves? Not one of us has ever made a real sacrifice. Not one of us has ever been hurt by anything we ever did for Christ.

V. WE NEED CONSECRATION

There is a pertinent question in *I Chronicles 29:5* — ". . . who then is willing to consecrate his service this day unto the Lord?" Only those who do will find happiness and power and usefulness in the Christian life. A famous preacher said, "I will cut myself off from all things that consume energy, time and money which do not have in them the redemptive element." I like that. He was simply saying that he was not going to spend his life on those things that do not count for God.

Here is a mighty pipe organ. A child can sit down and play "Chopsticks" on that organ with two fingers. But that does not portray all the possibilities wrapped up in that organ. It is possible for a great musician to bring forth beautiful music from it. God would like to use you and me to bless the world. But if we give Him only part of our lives, if we play with only two fingers, we fail Him. But if we will pull out all the stops and let Him play on all the keys of our lives, He will use us to bring forth music that will bless mankind.

John Ruskin said, "Anything which makes religion its second object makes religion no object. God will put up with a great many things in the human heart but there is one thing He will not put up with, and that is a divided heart. He who offers God a second place offers God no place at all."

Now what is the secret of a life of confidence, contentment, courage, cooperation and consecration? It is simply to love Christ supremely and surrender to Him completely.

A converted Indian was fervent in his praise and prayers and generous in his gifts. When someone asked him for the reason, he said, "Ah, you've never been in darkness as I was." Yes, we have been in the darkness of sin, but Christ the Great Light now has entered our hearts. As we walk in that Light let us love Him more and more. That is the greatest need of all.

9.

The Friend of God

James 2:23

The poorest man on the earth is the man who has no friends. I would feel badly indeed if I had to look out on the world and say, "I don't have one single friend anywhere." Friendship is a beautiful thing. He who has a true friend has found a pearl of great price. The man who is at the top of the ladder of success didn't get there by himself, he had to have friends to help him along the way. Poets and painters and musicians have told us about the beauty of friendship.

David and Jonathan were great friends. When Jonathan's own father sought to kill David, Jonathan took David's side and helped him to escape. . . . Ruth was the daughter-in-law of Naomi, yet they were wonderful friends who shared their sorrows and joys together. . . . Damon and Pythias were such friends that they were willing to die for each other. . . . Tennyson had a young friend named Arthur Henry Hallam. When the young man died Tennyson wrote his greatest poem in memory of him.

Yes, earthly friendships are fine and wonderful, but there is something more wonderful and that is friendship with God. In the Old Testament we find a man by the name of Abraham. God called him out of his everyday existence to give his life in service to the Lord. Years later James wrote about him and called him "the friend of God." Isn't it wonderful that God can say about a person, "He's my friend, she's my friend"?

I. The Grounds for This Friendship

1. *They trusted each other.* Abraham trusted God. When God called Abraham to leave his old home and go to a strange land, Abraham went out, not knowing where he was going nor what hardships awaited him. We would have asked, "Why should I go, what will you give me, when can I come back?" But Abraham just trusted God and went on.

Years went by and Abraham was an old man. The sorrow of his heart was that he had no children. But God had promised that he would have a son and Abraham trusted God and believed His promise. Fifty years went by before that son was born but Abraham trusted God to keep that promise. And in due time Isaac was born to Abraham and Sarah.

Then one day God told Abraham to take that boy, his only child, and offer him up as a sacrifice unto the Lord. Now God had promised that a great nation of people would spring from the loins of this son. But if Isaac were slain there would be no seed of Abraham. Still Abraham's faith did not waver. He believed that God would provide and would keep His promise. And God did just that. Isaac was saved and the nation of Israel was born. God is still making promises to His children. He may not fulfill them tomorrow or next week or next year. But we must be patient and wait on Him and trust Him. He "has never broken any promise spoken."

Not only did Abraham trust God, but God trusted Abraham. He said, "For I know him, that he will command his children and his household after him, and they shall keep the way of the Lord. . ." (Genesis 18:19). I wish He could say that of every mother and father today. Our children may forget what we say but they will never forget what we do. The memory of a good father's life or a good mother's Christianity has brought many a son and daughter back to God. I can say this out of years of experience. I have known men who were little and stingy and critical of the church and the things of God. And their children grew up with a distaste for the church and Christianity. Your influence as a Christian can be a deadly thing or a blessed thing. Be careful how you live, be careful of your influence.

2. *They communed with each other.* Abraham and God walked and talked together. God had planned to destroy Sodom and Gomorrah because of the sin which infested those wicked cities. And God said, "Shall I hide from Abraham that thing which I do?" (Genesis 18:17). He decided to reveal His plans to Abraham, so they talked together as friend to friend.

No friendship can thrive without some communication. You have a friend here in the city with whom you have almost daily communication. Then that friend moves to another city. For a while you write or call that friend quite often. Then there comes a time when communication ceases and that friendship dies. Now right here is where prayer comes in. We must live in daily communion with God if we expect to have a healthy and happy spiritual relationship with Him.

3. *They served each other.* God called upon Abraham to sacrifice his only son for Him and Abraham did not hesitate to obey God's call. And God turned about and gave up His only begotten Son, not only for Abraham, but for us all.

On one occasion the disciples said to Jesus, "We have left all to follow Thee, our homes, our families, our businesses, our friends. What are we going to get out of it?" And Jesus answered, "Follow me and you'll never lack for anything. I will repay you an hundred-fold in this world and in the world to come, life everlasting." If you are God's friend you will serve Him and He will serve you and reward you.

II. THE GUARANTEES OF THIS FRIENDSHIP

1. *This friendship guaranteed perfect security.* God said to Abraham, "Fear not, Abram: I am thy shield. . ." (Genesis 15: 1). The soldier used a shield for protection. Abraham had God for his shield. Abraham was rich, he lived among hostile tribes, who would have been very happy to take all that he had, his life was beset with many dangers. Yet for one hundred years Abraham was not molested. God cared for him.

He has made the same promise to us. If we trust Him He will protect us. The unseen presence hovers over all the children of God. As the mother hovers over her child and protects it, as the shepherd protects the sheep, so does God protect us.

2. *This friendship guaranteed success.* Abraham trusted God and followed Him and God prospered him. God never fails His friends. Now Abraham could not see all the success God was going to give him. God promised him a great nation but when Abraham died he had only one son and two grandsons. Four hundred years later the descendants of Abraham down in Egypt were like the sands of the sea in number. Abraham did become the father of a great nation and out of that nation came the Lord Jesus Christ.

The man who follows the Lord faithfully never fails. He may

not become rich but all of his needs will be supplied. David said, "I have been young, and now am old; yet have I not seen the righteous forsaken, nor his seed begging bread" (Psalm 37:25). And Jesus said, "But seek ye first the kingdom of God, and his righteousness; and all these things shall be added unto you" (Matthew 6:33).

3. *This friendship guaranteed perfect compensation.* God said to Abraham, ". . . I am thy exceeding great reward" (Genesis 15:1).

The time came when Abraham and his nephew, Lot, had some trouble. Both of them had large herds and there was not enough pasture room for both herds, so their herdsmen began to quarrel with each other. And Abraham graciously said, "Lot, here is all this land before us. You take your choice and I'll take what is left." Then Lot greedily took all the rich-looking land and Abraham took the sorry-looking land. You and I would have said, "Abraham, you'll be ruined. Your cattle will starve and Lot will get rich." But twenty years later Abraham was rich in flocks and herds and Lot was penniless. God always rewards His friends.

III. THE GLORY OF THIS FRIENDSHIP

There was nothing between Abraham and God and this made their friendship a glorious thing. When sin gets in the way our fellowship with God is broken.

Peter and Jesus were great friends. But one dark night Peter sinned against Jesus, he denied his Friend. However, because he did love Jesus, the time came when he wept his way back to Him. Only then did Peter find peace and joy. Is there anything between you and someone else? You'll never find peace until you do something about it. Is there anything between you and Jesus? There'll be no joy in your heart as long as that barrier remains. Get on your knees, confess that sin to God, get it out of the way. He is just waiting to forgive you and fill your heart with gladness.

Now as we walk and talk and live close to our friends we become like them. And as we walk with Jesus and talk with Him and live close to Him, we become more like Him. Oh, to be like Jesus! "More like the Master I would ever be" should be our constant prayer.

And someday by His grace, we are going to be exactly like Him. ". . . we shall be like him; for we shall see him as he is" (I John 3:2). A certain man went to see an artist. The artist was not at home, but his little daughter showed the visitor through the studio. Pointing to one picture, she said, "That is one of father's most beautiful pictures." Then they came to one picture containing only rough lines. The man smiled and asked, "Is this one beautiful, too?" And the little girl answered, "Yes, you can't see the beauty in it yet, but when my father finishes with it, it will be beautiful. He always paints beautiful pictures."

The Christian's life may not be beautiful now. There are too many sins, too many stains, too many flaws in the best of us. But when God finishes with us, we shall stand out in the beauty of the great King.

Dr. Ellis Fuller, one-time president of the Southern Baptist Theological Seminary, led a group of people through the Holy Land. On Saturday the group said to him, "Dr. Fuller, on Sunday morning we are going to Calvary and we want you to preach to us on the spot where Jesus was crucified." He said that the thought of this responsibility kept him awake most of the night. He tried to think of what he would say, but the words would not come. He didn't feel equal to preaching at the place where Jesus died. So he spent his waking moments memorizing the account of the crucifixion from Matthew's gospel.

The next morning they walked out to Calvary together. Not a word was spoken, everything was as quiet as death. When the time came for him to speak Dr. Fuller turned his face toward heaven and quoted the scripture picturing the crucifixion. The people sobbed and the tears ran down their cheeks. Then the preacher said, "Right there is where He died for you and me." He then quoted Isaac Watt's hymn:

> When I survey the wondrous cross,
> On which the Prince of Glory died,
> My richest gain I count but loss,
> And pour contempt on all my pride.
>
> Forbid it, Lord, that I should boast,
> Save in the death of Christ, my God;
> All the vain things that charm me most,
> I sacrifice them to His blood.

> See, from His head, His hands, His feet,
> Sorrow and love flow mingled down;
> Did e'er such love and sorrow meet,
> Or thorns compose so rich a crown?
>
> Were the whole realm of nature mine,
> That were a present far too small;
> Love so amazing, so divine,
> Demands my soul, my life, my all.

And as they turned away from Calvary they said they felt that if they had a thousand lives, they would want to give them all for Him who purchased their salvation with His blood. Don't you feel the same way?

Isn't Jesus a wonderful friend? Don't you love Him? Don't you want to get a little closer to Him? Don't you want to give Him your very life?

10.

God's Outstanding Man
Acts 27:9-10, 21-37

Paul was a prisoner because of his loyalty to Christ. Now since he had appealed to Caesar he was being taken to Rome to appear before the Emperor. The voyage over the Mediterranean was being taken in the worst time of the year. However, the captain of the ship seemed to know that Paul was not just an ordinary prisoner so he gave him certain liberties on the ship. And Paul took it upon himself to advise the captain not to sail. But the captain ignored this advice, set sail and ran into one of the worst storms described in the Bible.

They were in great danger for many days, fearing for their lives and the ship. The sun and stars were not seen and the tempest swept them backward and forward at its will. Then one day Paul practically assumed command. He said to the passengers and crew, "God has spoken to me and has told me what is going to happen. The ship will be destroyed, but no harm will come to us. We will arrive safely on shore." Then Paul advised them what action to take. They followed his advice this time and finally arrived at Melita. The ship was broken to pieces, but all those on board were safe.

There were 276 men on the ship, but who was the outstanding man on board? It was not the captain, not the pilot, not the centurion, but the little preacher named Paul, a humble follower of Jesus Christ. In times of crisis an outstanding man is always needed, someone to take over, to make decisions, to guide others. These are the men who keep the world going. They lead our churches, our schools, our nation. Paul was the outstanding man on the ship. Let us look at some of the qualifications of God's man.

I. God's Man Thinks Prayerfully

Here we see Paul as he studies the weather. He thought that this was the wrong time to sail. He was always like this. He didn't rush into things without thinking them out and praying about them. When he was knocked down and blinded on the Damascus Road, he had three days of blindness in which to think things over and this changed the whole course of his life. Then he did not rush into the ministry. He spent two years in Arabia, alone with God and his thoughts.

Thinking men are needed today. Just take the spiritual realm, for example. On every side there are hundreds of nice people who are on the road to hell. Why? Because they never give any thought to their spiritual condition before God. If they would only stop and think they would say, "I know I am not right with God. I know that someday I must die and face the judgment and I know I ought to make some preparation for that day." But they go on in life, pursuing worldly things and neglecting their eternal welfare.

Then there are hundreds of Christians, church members, who never go to church, who never give to the Lord, who live as if they had never met Christ. They ought to stop and think about what the Lord has done for them. Out of their gratitude they should say, "No longer will I neglect my Christian duty. I'll show God my gratitude by giving Him my best service."

Why is it that so many of our people go off into some of the rotten, unbiblical "isms" and cults? It is because they don't think things out. If they did think they would say, "This is not true to God's Word, therefore it can't be right."

Sometime ago a woman in Texas had a son who was accused of a crime. She made this promise to God, "If you will let my son be acquitted, I will walk 387 miles to the city to honor the Virgin Mary." Her son was acquitted and she began the long trek. A priest gave her permission to ride in a car for the last part of the journey. Oh, the pity of it! If such people would just stop and think and read the Word of God, they would know that they owe nothing to a statue of Mary. They need only to get down on their knees and thank God.

Bacon said that "knowledge is power," and the Bible says, "My people are destroyed for lack of knowledge. . ." (Hosea 4:6). So God's man seeks knowledge from God. Then when he obtains that knowledge he acts accordingly. Paul had a word from God and he acted intelligently.

II. God's Man Has a Simple, Childlike Faith

In the midst of the storm the experienced seamen gave up hope. But Paul said, "I believe God will do what He said." The Bible says that "without faith it is impossible to please God." Noah had faith. He built the ark and it pleased God. Abraham had faith. He went out, not knowing where he was going, and it pleased God. Moses had faith. He gave up the riches and prestige of Egypt and it pleased God. Gideon had faith. He led a small army to victory and it pleased God. Daniel had faith. His prayer life brought him to the lions' den but it pleased God.

Dwight L. Moody was in a certain city to begin a revival. He believed God would bless the meeting, so he stood before the great audience and said, "Let us bow our heads and thank God for what He is going to do for us." Men who have faith please God. God always rewards faith. ". . . According to your faith be it unto you" (Matthew 9:29).

III. God's Man Has a Sane Optimism Based on the Word of God

Paul stood on deck, facing death, with the angry seas beating against the boat. "Be of good cheer," he said. "You have been fasting for 14 days, now it would be best for your health to eat something." Now we see that his optimism was based on faith. If I say, "I know that things will work out all right," that optimism must be based on faith, faith that a great God will cause them to work out all right.

Often we are pessimistic about our work in the church and the progress of the cause of Christ. Someone has said that "instead of advancing in the face of difficulties, we look for an avenue of retreat. Instead of being inspired by the spirit of self-sacrifice, we recline in self-ease. Instead of prayerfully considering the world's needs and giving according to our means, we consider ourselves and give according to our meanness. Instead of being loyal to the pastor and praying for him to succeed, we kick him and demand a change. Instead of saying that something should be done, we give 45 reasons as to why it can't be done. Instead of scattering sunshine, we find a fly in every ointment and criticize everything."

Yes, we need to develop the spirit of optimism, based upon the precious promises of God. In November 1918 Teddy Roosevelt cast his last vote. He was suffering from rheumatism and his right foot was badly swollen. When he came to the voting booth someone asked him how he was feeling. He replied, "I'm all wrong in the feet, but all right in the head." He was showing optimism in the face of suffering.

Dr. J. D. Jones was a prominent preacher of another day. He made a trip through some Canadian woods where there were no birds. He wrote home saying, "The woods and mountains are beautiful and majestic, but I miss one thing. They are songless." That's the way it is with some Christians. They say that they are trusting Christ, but they have lost their song, they have no joy, no gladness in their lives. This causes the world to think that Christianity is a useless religion. But the real Christian, with a Saviour who has washed away his sin, with a God of all power, with the Holy Spirit dwelling within him, has the right to be optimistic.

IV. God's Man Is a Reverent and Grateful Man

Paul took bread, and lifting up his eyes toward heaven, gave thanks in the presence of them all. They were not Christians, but this did not keep Paul from offering thanks. Today men rush to work, to eat, to play, to church, but they forget to pray. Oh, the sin of a prayerless life. Jesus was reverent, the angels were reverent, the saints of God have always been reverent. So should we be.

A group of literary men met one day in a London clubroom. They began to talk about the illustrious men of the past. One of them asked, "What would you do if Milton walked into this room?" And one of them answered, "We would give him an ovation that would compensate for the lack of recognition he received when he was on the earth." Then the question was asked, "What would you do if Shakespeare walked in?" And another answered, "We would arise and crown him as master of literature and song." Then the question was asked, "What would you do if Jesus Christ walked in?" And Charles Lamb answered, "I think we would all fall on our faces at His feet." This is the spirit that every Christian should have as he approaches the things of God.

V. God's Man Is the Master of Himself

Paul took over the mastery of the situation, because he was master of himself. Solomon said, ". . . he that ruleth his spirit [is better] than he that taketh a city" (Proverbs 16:32). The greatest battlefield is in the human heart and the human spirit, the greatest battles occur there, the greatest victories are won there. A man came to my office seeking financial help. But when I smelled liquor on his breath, I knew that he needed something more than financial aid, he needed to get mastery over himself.

How can one gain mastery of himself? Only through Jesus Christ. Men make their vows, they sign pledges, they make promises. But they fail because they have no divine power to help them. One morning a doctor called me and said, "There's a man in St. Mary's Hospital. He is a prominent citizen, but he has been drinking and ruining his life and his business. He wants you to come and bring your Bible, so that he can put his hand on it and swear that he'll never drink again." I went to the hospital and allowed the man to do that and I prayed by his bedside. But I told him that his vow was not enough and that he could not keep it in himself. I told him that he needed to yield himself to Christ and enlist God's help in his battle. But this he would not do. In a few months he was drinking again. In a few more months he was dead.

Dr. J. Wilbur Chapman was holding a meeting in a certain place and a drunkard came to hear him preach. The only seat left was on the front row and the man took that seat right in front of the preacher. He heard the Gospel and the Holy Spirit deeply convicted him of his sin. He saw his great need of the Saviour and went forward, trusting his all to Christ. Later on the temptation to drink came upon him again and again, but when it did he would run as fast as possible to his home, where he fell upon his knees by the bedside and prayed for strength to overcome. Before long the victory was won. Yes, the only way to mastery is through Christ.

VI. God's Man Is a Helpful Man

Paul was a great help to all those on the ship. They came to depend upon him and he did not fail them. Many people live only for self, they never help anyone. What contribution are they making toward humanity? I heard a woman say, "I have helped others and I got nothing in return but trouble." Sometimes this seems to be true. The ones that we help most often turn against us. But I have learned that in the end some blessing comes that we would not otherwise receive. Listen to this poem from an unknown author:

> He never saw the trouble, he only saw the deed.
> He never thought of distance, his mind was on the need.
> He never reckoned money as a prize worth clinging to.
> He said its only value was the good that it could do.
>
> He never stopped to reckon what he'd miss, of joy, to stay
> And help a fellow-being who was stranded on the way,
> Never paused to think of pleasures that he'd cherished long
>   and planned,
> All he saw was one in trouble who must have a helping
>   hand.
>
> There seemed nothing so important that he wouldn't turn
>   aside
> For the man who needed friendship and was really trouble-
>   tried;
> He wasn't one to answer, "I have something else to do."
> He thought his foremost duty was to help a man he knew.
>
> He never saw the trouble, he only saw the deed.
> He never thought of sacrifice, his mind was on the need.
> He had this simple motto which he followed to the end,
> "When the other man's in trouble, that's the time to be his
>   friend."

Yes, Paul was God's outstanding man. You and I can never be as great as Paul, but we can seek to acquire these outstanding qualities. We are to:

1. Think prayerfully and act intelligently.
2. Have a simple childlike faith.
3. Have a sane optimism based on the Word of God.
4. Have a reverent and grateful spirit.
5. Gain mastery over self through Christ.
6. Help others along life's pathway.

At the end of that voyage Paul proved to be the outstanding man, while the name of the captain has long been forgotten.

And you and I, if we will faithfully follow Christ, can take our place at the end of the journey with Paul and that glorious band of saints who dared to become the followers of the Saviour.

Psalm 37 gives us a motto for life. We are to commit our way unto the Lord, we are to trust also in Him. Then He will bring to pass the very best things for us. We don't know about tomorrow and the days or years to come but we can trust God and commit all our days and ways to Him, knowing that He will surely bring us safely through all of life and home at the end of the journey.

11.

The Marks of a Christian — Loyalty

Galatians 6:17;
Revelation 2:10

As a setting for this series of talks, I want you to look at a picture. Paul said, ". . . I bear in my body the marks of the Lord Jesus" (Galatians 6:17). He was in prison at this time. Chains were about his ankles, but his soul was free. He was a prisoner of Caesar, but he was a free man in Christ Jesus. He was in bondage to the Roman Empire, yet Christ was his only master.

There he sits in prison writing this letter to the Galatians. He wants to use a striking illustration to show them that he belongs to Christ. He notices that everything around him is marked with the sign of the Imperial Caesar. He saw this sign upon his prison clothes, upon the eating utensils, upon his chains. The hand of the guard was stamped with the initial of the Emperor, declaring to the world whose he was. Now Paul said, "I have some marks branded on me. They are the marks of the Lord Jesus." He could roll up his sleeve and show the mark he had received at Philippi. Upon his shoulder he could show the scar that he received when they stoned him at Lystra. He was boldly saying, "These things show that I belong to Christ. I have His mark upon me." These were physical marks, but surely the great apostle bore many spiritual marks, also.

I want to take this figure for this series of talks. We ought to have marks upon us as Christians, declaring that we belong to Christ. If we do not have these marks, we are not bearing fruit in the Christian life. Now the first of these marks is *loyalty*.

I. LOYALTY EXEMPLIFIED

1. *We see it exemplified in Paul.* From the moment he met Christ on the Damascus Road until the time his head rolled off

the block, he was loyal. He could have saved himself from suffering and death. He could have been a man of fame, lauded and honored. But Christ meant more to him than all the world. Though men might tempt him to deny Christ, he could always say, "You may burn my body, you may sacrifice me upon your altars, but I will still be true to Christ." Oh, how we need such men as Paul today, men who are loyal to Christ and to the highest and best things of life.

2. *We see loyalty exemplified in Jesus.* All of these marks which we will talk about are found in Jesus. And the marks that were in Jesus should be found in every Christian. First, He was loyal to His heavenly Father. He said, "Lo, I come to do thy will, O God. . ." (Hebrews 10:9). Great temptations came to Him, but nothing could turn Him aside from the purpose of His life. He was loyal from the cradle to the grave. If we follow in His train, we must be loyal to God. Loyalty to God means loyalty to His mission for our lives.

Then Jesus was loyal to His friends. We remember that Peter denied Him with an oath. But Jesus still loved him and sent him a special message, asking that he meet Him at the old trysting place. As Jesus was loyal to His disciples, so is He loyal to us. Never has He broken one promise that He has made to us. There are many others we might name who have been loyal. Every great man has been a man of loyalty.

II. Loyalty Needed

1. *We need loyalty in the state.* Loyalty is opposite to lawlessness. Was there ever such a time of lawlessness as the present time? If you are loyal to your country, you will obey its laws. You will obey them even though you don't like them.

2. *We need loyalty in the home.* Our homes are not building the men and women they once did. There was a time when the memory of home would cause a man to walk a straight path. But the bars have been let down. There is little respect for authority in the homes of today. Our homes need to be loyal to the great principles of truth and right and we need to train our young people in these principles. Our homes must be the kind of places which grow character and Christian manhood and womanhood.

3. *We need loyalty in the church.* We have millions of names on our church rolls today, but very few members put the church at the center of their lives. Their loyalty is given to the things of the world. When they are called upon to do something in the church, they are too busy with worldly organizations. If we would give more loyalty to Christ's church, men would realize the value of Christianity. These words were carved over a European fort, "We will die under these ruins rather than surrender." The church is our fort and our battleground. We should be willing to die under its ruins rather than surrender.

4. *We need loyalty in the little things of life.* If a man is never faithful in the little things, he will never be faithful in the big things. A girl can commit a small act of immodesty and that disloyalty will lead to bigger sins. A boy can be just a little bit dishonest and that dishonesty may lead to embezzle-ment of a large sum. If a man is not loyal in tithing when he makes $50.00 a week, he won't be loyal when he makes $500.00 a week. A preacher saw one of his members gambling at a winter resort. The member said, "I was just playing for small stakes, five cents per point." If it is wrong to gamble, it is wrong to gamble for small stakes or large. We must not sur-render our principles. We must be loyal in the little things of life.

5. *We need to be loyal to our convictions.* Our convictions should be based upon the teachings of the Bible, and we should be loyal to them. Moses was loyal as he faced Pharaoh. Pharaoh was a big man. Why didn't Moses surrender to him? It was because he had a conviction that he must speak the truth for God, unpleasant as it might be. His loyalty helped to make him the greatest man in the Old Testament. I see John the Baptist out yonder by the riverside, preaching repentance. Some rich Pharisees come to listen to his sermon. Does he lower his standards? No, he said, "O generation of vipers, who hath warned you to flee from the wrath to come?" (Matthew 3:7). He stood up for his convictions even though it cost him his life. I see Paul yonder on Mars Hill. He notices that the Athenians are worshiping many gods, even having a statue erected to the Unknown God. Did he join them? Did he put aside his loyalties? No, he stood before that group and said, "I worship the one true God."

Loyalty to your convictions will often bring you into conflict. A boy talked to his pastor and said, "I am greatly perplexed. My employer wants me to do a thing which I cannot rightfully do. If I do not do this, I will lose my job. I am the only support of my mother. What must I do?" The pastor replied, "It is not a question of your loyalty to your mother or your employer. It is a question of your loyalty to your conscience and to Christ. Satisfy that and these other things will work out all right." Whatever the cost, let us be true to our highest convictions.

6. *We need to be loyal to Christ.* The secret of a good life is to have some great power to whom one pays loyalty. We must get back to loyalty to Christ. We are His by creation and redemption. He owns us. His mark is stamped upon us. We must be loyal to Him. This means that we will be loyal to His principles and His teachings. I am afraid that many people come to church and learn about His principles, yet they forget these principles when they go out into the marketplaces of life. They forget the golden rule. They forget to put Christ before self. During World War II President Roosevelt said, "We must be Americans and nothing else." You and I, if we have the marks of Christ upon us, must be Christians and nothing else. We need to put loyalty to Christ above all else.

III. Loyalty Rewarded

1. *There is the reward of receiving greater light.* When you are loyal to a friend, you are constantly learning more about his nature. If you are disloyal to him, he shuts himself up to you. If you are loyal to Christ, He will be continually revealing Himself to you. The more loyal you are to Him, the more you will know about Him. Men who are not loyal to Him know very little about Jesus, the Bible or Christian character. The song expresses the desire, "More About Jesus Would I Know." When we are loyal we come to know more about Him.

2. *There is the reward of greater usefulness.* The more faithful we are, the more He will give us to do. ". . . thou hast been faithful over a few things, I will make thee ruler over many things. . ." (Matthew 25:23). When a man is loyal in business, he is promoted to greater positions of usefulness. This

is also true in the Kingdom of God. Certainly you don't want to be a baby Christian all your life. We grow through loyalty.

3. *There is the reward of the Master's approval.* Jesus will never say, "Well done, thou good and faithful servant" to the disloyal people, to those who live on the fringe of a good Christian life. Before I entered the ministry I worked for a fine concern in the South. One morning the manager came in to see me and said, "I want to congratulate you upon the fine work you have done and the good results you have achieved." I appreciated that. But, oh, how much greater to hear Jesus say, "You have been loyal. You have done well."

When our soldiers returned from the battlefront, we cheered them because of their loyalty and their good deeds. And when the saints of God march down the heavenly streets, the Master will praise them because they have been faithful to Him. The rewards of heaven always go to the faithful.

In New York City there is the bronze statue of a man. His arms are bound, his feet are tied. At the base of the statue we read these words, "I regret that I have only one life to give to my country." These were the words of Nathan Hale. Oh, let us be loyal to Christ, and the best of life. Then our only regret will be that we have but one life to give to Him who loved us and died for us.

12.

The Marks of a Christian — Courage

Galatians 6:17;
Acts 14:19-22

We are still talking about the marks of a Christian. Our last message was on loyalty. Now we think about courage. This is an essential mark of a Christian. It takes real courage to live the Christian life. Paul wrote these words while he was in prison, declaring that he had upon him the marks of the Lord Jesus.

I. Examples of Courage

1. *The courage of Paul.* Paul was stoned at Lystra and left for dead, but God performed a miracle. He was not through with Paul. He gave him a complete recovery. What will Paul do now? Surely it would be foolish for him to return to the place of defeat. But he could say, "I am not defeated. I take pleasure in these things for Christ's sake." He was not discouraged. He went right on back to work facing the same mob that had stoned him. Showing a splendid courage, he was ready to do a mighty work there.

Later on we find him in prison in Caesarea. When King Agrippa came to town, Festus told him about Paul. The king was interested in Paul and had him brought before him. He was told that he could speak for himself. However, instead of doing this, he spoke for the Lord Jesus. It took a mighty courage for him to stand before the king and his court and preach the One whom they hated. But he did preach in such an effective way that Agrippa was greatly impressed. He cried out, "Almost thou persuadest me to be a Christian" (Acts 26:28). It takes real courage to stand before a hostile crowd and say, "I am for Christ."

2. *The courage of John the Baptist.* He called the religious leaders of His day a "generation of vipers." Later he found King

78

Herod living in sin with his brother's wife. What a courageous scene we look upon as John the Baptist faced Herod. Here is the king, arrayed in royal robes, with the woman sitting by his side. Here is John clothed in camel's hair. He is a simple country preacher. What does he say? Will he bow down and sanction all that the king is doing? No, he had more courage than that. He pointed his finger at the king and said to him, "It is not lawful for thee to have her." He was placed in prison and later beheaded. It took courage for him to denounce the king as a sinner, but he had that courage.

3. *The courage of Caleb and Joshua.* God commanded Moses to select twelve men and send them into Canaan as spies. When they returned, ten of the spies said, "It is a good land, but the people up there are giants, and we are but grasshoppers in their sight. We are not able to take the land." But Caleb and Joshua were men of another spirit. They said, "With God's help we can take the land. Let us not fear the people, for we know that the Lord will be with us." They were men of real courage and they were rewarded for that courage. The other men died in the wilderness, but Caleb and Joshua entered into the Promised Land.

4. *The courage of Jesus.* Oh, how courageous He was! He stood before howling mobs and faced the stoutest opposition, yet He was not afraid. He stood up before the mighty leaders of the Sanhedrin. He ran the money changers out of the temple. He was a real man of courage. When Herod sent a message to Him, threatening to kill Him, He said, "Go and tell the old fox that I am busy today and tomorrow. Tell him that though he has great power, I am not afraid of him." This took real courage. . . . In the Garden of Gethsemane, when the mob came out to arrest Him, He said, "I am the One whom you seek." They fell back to the ground in the face of such courage. His followers need the same courage today, the courage to stand fast in the face of the world.

II. The Need of Courage

1. *We need courage in church life.* Why do men give excuses for not being active in the church? Maybe it is because they don't have sufficient courage. Religion is not easy, it is not a

bed of roses. It takes courage to face the demands and responsibilities of the Christian life. We sing the song, "Like a mighty army, Moves the Church of God." Yet we see some Christians moving, not like a mighty army, but like a hospital full of crippled children. They are in the church and enjoying its comforts, but the burdens fall upon others. Many Christians are like an elevator. Step into the elevator and without any effort on your own part, you are carried to the next floor. Some people feel that the church is an elevator and all they need to do is to step into it, and they will be carried to heaven without any effort. But we will never have any great Christian courage while we are resting on someone else.

2. *We need courage to stand for the right.* It is easy to stand for the things that are right while you are inside the church. But can you say, "No" out in the world? When someone suggests doing a wrong thing, do you say, "I'll do it to get in with the crowd"? Or can you say, "I am a Christian and I will not do that"? When they have an office party where you work and the liquor is passed around, can you turn it down? Do you have that much courage? We need enough courage to stand up for our convictions wherever we are.

3. *We need courage in the ordinary duties of life.* There are two kinds of courage. One kind is for critical occasions, and the other kind is for everyday life. It is in the last category that we fail. It takes courage to plod along every day, carrying life's responsibilities, and always standing up for the right. A man who won many medals from his country for bravery in battle came home and remained drunk most of the time. He had the courage to face the enemy on the battlefield, but he had not the courage to master himself. Ordinary courage is the greatest kind, and it is the kind we need today. Another man who won the Croix de Guerre refused it, saying, "Let me go home and make good there first, then I will accept the medal." He realized that it took more courage to live in everyday life than it did to fight in battle.

Captain Scott and a group of men went to the South Pole. The weather was far below zero. Their feet were practically frozen. They were about to drop down in the snow to die, but Captain Scott kept saying, "Slog on, slog on!" And they made the grade. This is the kind of courage we need. In the face of a mutinous crew, Columbus cried out, "Sail on, sail on, sail on!" Just sailing on the right track is what we need.

There will be many times when we are going to be afraid, but we must take courage and go ahead. It is said that King Henry IV was a great soldier, but his knees always trembled just before battle. Then he would say to them, "Tremble, you vile things! You would tremble more than that if you knew where I am going to carry you in the next half hour." It is hard always to live rightly for Christ, and it is easy to give up, but we must grit our teeth and go ahead.

A swimmer gave up in the middle of a race and his coach asked him why he had given up. He answered, "I got some sand in my mouth." Then the coach blasted out, "You ought to have swallowed it. You need some in your system." We certainly need anything that will give us courage in the Christian race.

III. How Can We Get This Courage?

1. *By realizing the presence of God.* When we are afraid then we must remember that ". . . If God be for us, who can be against us?" (Romans 8:31). One day a great army came forth to capture Elisha. His servant looked around him and was filled with fear. He expressed that fear to Elisha in no uncertain terms. Then Elisha prayed, asking God to open the young man's eyes. His prayer was answered, the young man's eyes were opened and he saw the hosts of heaven encamped round about them. God's power is always around those who trust in Him.

When Paul was on shipboard and the ship was battling against the storm, he took command of the situation. He said to the passengers, ". . . be of good cheer [courage] . . ." (Acts 27:25). How could he feel that way in the face of impending disaster? He answered the question for himself, "For there stood by me this night the angel of God . . . saying, Fear not . . ." (Acts 27:23, 24). He sensed the presence of God. "The angel of the LORD encampeth round about them that fear him, and delivereth them" (Psalm 34:7). We depend too much upon ourselves. No wonder we lose courage. We need to realize that God is near and that "all things work together for good to them that love God."

2. *By having a great faith in our cause.* During the war someone asked this question, "Why does a certain regiment always conquer, while others fail?" And the answer given was, "This conquering regiment had great faith in their cause while others did not." We have a great cause, we have a great Captain. We are on the winning team. We can always have courage when we know that Christ is with us and will bring us through.

3. *By having hope for the future.* We can bear up bravely when we have hope. Where there is no hope, courage is gone. Amundsen said that after his men reached the South Pole they had nothing else to look forward to. They became discouraged and disgruntled. Hope keeps a man alive. Hope makes a man brave as he faces the future. Hope sustains a sick person as he looks forward to the morning.

The word "courage" comes from the Latin word "cor" which means heart. Courage is a matter of the heart. Let us put our heart close up to Jesus Christ and He will give us the courage to live the Christian life.

The Waldensians lost their leader when he was a young man in his early thirties. However, because of his hard work in their behalf, his hair was white as the driven snow. When they gathered to say good-by to him, one of the men touched the young leader's hair and said, "Our comrade's hair became white because of his loyalty to our cause." This statement brought a great cheer from the Waldensians and sent them out to fight for their cause. Let us be brave and courageous and others will be helped and strengthened and inspired to take up the Christian life.

13.

The Marks of a Christian — Patience

Galatians 6:17;
James 1:4

The third mark of a Christian is that of patience. We have already studied about loyalty and courage. We certainly do need patience today, since we are going at such a rapid rate through life. Now, what is patience? The word literally means "willing to suffer." It means self-control, it means the ability to wait and not to rush into things. We need patience today in the home, in business, in school, in the church. The motto today seems to be "make it snappy." We even want to streamline our Sunday church services.

I. SOME EXAMPLES OF PATIENCE

1. *Paul was patient.* He tells us that he had a thorn in the flesh. We do not know what this thorn was. There have been many guesses about the matter. Some say that it was a hot temper. Some say that it was the opposition given his work by his enemies. Some say that it was eye trouble. Whatever it was, we know that it gave him much trouble. He prayed for God to remove the thorn. He prayed earnestly three times. Then God seemed to whisper to him, "I will not remove the thorn, but I will give you grace sufficient to bear it." Paul then learned to say, "I will keep the thorn. It is better to have the thorn and God's added grace than to have no thorn and lesser grace." So we see all along how patient Paul was.

Do you have a thorn in the flesh? Do you have a cross to bear? Then ask God to do what is best about it. He may not remove the thorn, He may not take away the cross, but He will help you by giving you added grace.

2. *Moses was patient.* God placed him over two million people. How dull they were! How unfaithful! The minute Moses

83

turned his back, they made a golden calf and bowed down to worship it. But through the years of his leadership, Moses never quit. He was always patient with the children of Israel.

3. *Jesus was patient.* His disciples never did understand Him until after His resurrection. Many times He had to say to them, "You do not yet understand." Yet he never lost patience. For three and a half years Judas and Peter walked with Him. Judas betrayed Him and Peter denied Him. But Jesus was still patient. Some of our teachers today become impatient because their pupils are so dull. But not so with Jesus. He was always patient. At the wedding of Cana He said, ". . . mine hour is not yet come" (John 2:4). Many times others wanted to force the issue upon Him, but He was patient. He knew how to wait until the proper hour.

He was patient at His trial. Not one word of bitterness did He utter. He was patient right through all His suffering. He was patient as He hung on the cross. Oh, if we are to be like Jesus we must be Christlike in our patience!

II. QUALITIES OF PATIENCE

1. *Patience means the ability to wait.* During the war the hardest hour that our soldiers had to live through was the zero hour, the hour just before a charge was to be made. It is important to know how to wait and not to rush headlong into anything. There is a psychological moment for everything. If you do anything before that moment, you only complicate matters. When we spend our energy in restless and useless activity, we are only wasting the strength we will need when the time of battle comes.

The poet tells us to "learn to labor and to wait." Many of us have learned to labor, but we have not learned to wait. Several years ago there was a mine disaster in a western state. Several men were trapped below the surface. No one knew whether they were dead or alive. Mothers and wives and children gathered at the mouth of the pits, where they could do nothing but wait. The nervous strain was so great that many of them collapsed. But when the first news came up from the mine those waiting loved ones scurried off for blankets. It was a relief for them to be active again.

Milton, the blind author, said, "They also serve who only stand and wait." Yes, those who wait serve as much as those who go forth to battle, but it is harder on them. We need to learn today to wait. We must not rush ahead of God. *Isaiah 40:31* says, "But they that wait upon the LORD shall renew their strength; they shall mount up with wings as eagles; they shall run, and not be weary; and they shall walk, and not faint."

2. *Patience means resignation.* We must not curse our fate, but we must resign ourselves to the will of God. The story is told of a man who visited an institution for the deaf and dumb. He would write out a question on the blackboard, and then one of the students would come forward and write the answers. Finally he wrote a cruel question upon the board. It was this, "If God loved you, why did He make you as you are?" When the question was read the children all over the room began to sob. Then one little girl went up to the blackboard and wrote this answer, "Even so, Father: for so it seemed good in thy sight" (Matthew 11:26). That is a perfect example of resignation. Job said, "Though he slay me, yet will I trust in him . . ." (Job 13:15). Jesus said in Gethsemane, ". . . not my will, but thine, be done (Luke 22:42). "If I must go to the cross, I am ready."

A woman who had been in a serious accident was confined to her bed for many weeks. One day she said to the doctor, "How long must I lie here helpless?" And the doctor answered, "Just one day at a time." And it helped her to know that every day God would care for her through that day and give her strength for every hour.

Sir Harry Lauder was singing at a theater in London when he received the sad news that his only son had been killed in battle. He finished his performance at the theater, then went home to Scotland and to his wife. Smiling through their tears they sought to help one another. Upon their knees they prayed and asked God to give them grace and comfort. They did not complain to God, they simply asked for His help. They were resigned to God's will and His help came to them. Yes, patience sometimes means resignation.

3. *Patience means endurance.* In recent years we have had many silly endurance contests in America. These are not worth

while. We need strength to endure the daily grind of life. In business only five men out of one hundred reach complete success, we are told. The others have not learned to stick it out. Many people join our churches, but they do not endure. They make their pledges and their vows to God and they keep them only a short time. We need to learn the lesson of endurance in every walk of life.

III. Some Cases Where Patience Is Necessary

1. *We need patience in the presence of life's mysteries.* Some people throw religion out the window because they cannot understand all of its mysteries. Some smart-alecks in college told a professor that they did not believe that man had a soul, since you could not see nor hear nor smell nor touch nor taste it. The professor wisely answered, "Did you ever see a pain? Did you ever hear one? Did you ever smell one? Did you ever touch one? Did you ever taste one? Yet we know that there is such a thing as pain."

We simply don't have the capacity to receive some things. Jesus said to His disciples, "I have yet many things to say unto you, but ye cannot bear them now" (John 16:12). We ought to leave the mysteries with God. We ought to be willing to let Him know more than we know. So we are to be patient. We are to trust God. We are to take the mysteries on faith. Then some day in the golden glow of that better land, we will sit down beside the Lord Jesus and He will explain to us all of the mysteries of life. Then we will see that many of the things which were so hard down here were simply blessings in disguise which God sent to us for our good and His glory.

2. *We need patience when we are under a great disappointment.* We plan big things and when they fall through our hearts are broken. That is the time to be patient. That is the time to take up the cross and follow Christ. Often when men are defeated they give up and quit. But when we have the right kind of patience, we accept the disappointments of life. We "gird up our loins" and we tackle the job which awaits us. Even when the greatest disappointment comes, the Christian can always remember that "all things work together for good to them that love God . . ." (Romans 8:28).

3. *We need patience when things are moving slowly.* The parent is patient with the dull child. The teacher is patient with the backward pupil. God is patient with us. We need to be patient when things are not moving as swiftly as we think they ought to move. Some years ago I visited the Endless Caverns in Virginia. The guide told us that the stalactites and stalagmites grew only one inch in a hundred years. Then I said to myself, "Why can't I be patient in doing the Lord's work, remembering that He will bring forth the results He wants to bring forth?" Often we cannot see much progress in our Christian work, but we must be patient and keep on plodding and God will give the increase.

A certain wealthy woman, dressed in simple clothing, made it a practice to do welfare work among the poor of her city. She carried clothing and food and medicine to many a needy home. One day after she had been in one of these homes, a little girl looked up into her face and said, "Lady, are you Jesus' wife?" I wonder if people think of Jesus when they look at us. I wonder if they feel that we are this near to Him. Oh, let us live a patient, godly life, then men will know that we have a secret within. They will know that we are akin to Jesus and that we follow Him.

14.

The Marks of a Christian — Humility

Galatians 6:17;
Luke 14:7-11

In this series we have already spoken of loyalty, courage and patience. Now let us think of humility as the fourth mark of the Christian. Before Christ came into the world the worst thing that could be said about a man was that he was humble. This was considered to be a quality of a slave. A free man would be insulted to be called humble. But since Jesus came the best thing that you can say about a man is that he is humble. There is so much selfishness in the world, and so few who are truly humble. How we do need more humility today. This is certainly a Christ-like quality and the more we have of it, the more Christ-like we are.

Today men can talk hours about themselves and they are always the hero of their own stories. They never tell the tales about the times in which they were the "goat." A ball player talks about his home runs and the tremendous catches that he made, but never about his errors and his strike-outs. When some men give a little money to a charitable cause, this gift is often brought up in their conversation. When he carries food to a poor family he will soon tell you about it. I have often visited men who talked for a long time about what they had done in the church and for the Lord, but they say nothing about what the Lord has done for them. Humility is needed everywhere, but most of all in our service for Christ. Too many Christian workers want the high places. If you don't permit them to be "the whole show," they become peeved and quit.

A young man applied to a mission board, stating that he wanted to go to China as a missionary. The board members felt that he would not be a suitable missionary, but he was so enthusiastic they hated to turn him down. They asked him this question, "Would you like to go as a servant?" And he enthusiastically replied, "I will go as a hewer of wood, a carrier of water, or anything, if you will only let me serve the cause of Christ." I wonder how many of our church members have a spirit like that. How many of them would give up a place of prominence to take an obscure place in the service of Christ?

A neatly dressed young man came to Mr. Wanamaker and asked for a job. He was told that no jobs were open, but he said, "I am willing to do anything." Mr. Wanamaker thought he would get rid of him, and so he said to him, "I could give you a job washing windows." Quickly the young man said, "I will take it." He washed those windows as they had never been washed before and the time came when he was manager of the store and making $100,000 per year. We need that kind of people in the service of Christ today. "He that humbleth himself shall be exalted, and he that exalteth himself shall be humbled."

I. SOME EXAMPLES OF HUMILITY

1. *The humility of Paul.* The great apostle boasted only about one thing. His glory was in the cross of Christ. He did not talk about what he had done for Jesus, but always he talked about what the Saviour had done for him. He had the privilege of leading Philemon to Christ. Philemon was evidently a wealthy man. Later Paul was in jail in Rome and it was in Rome that he led one of Philemon's slaves to Christ. His name was Onesimus. Paul took the slave to his heart as a brother. He sent him back to his master and interceded for him by saying, "If he . . . oweth thee aught, put that on mine account" (Philemon 18). Only a fine humility and real Christianity would have caused Paul to condescend in this manner.

2. *The humility of Moses.* Moses has been called the meekest man in the Bible. He was chosen of God to lead a great number of people toward the Promised Land. From the human standpoint, he had a right to be proud. But think of his humility. He went up on the mountaintop and talked with God and when he came back down, his face was shining like the sunlight. However, we read that he "wist not that the skin of his face shone . . ." (Exodus 34:30). He was so humble that he knew nothing of the glory shining in his own face.

3. *The humility of Jesus.* Jesus was the central figure in heaven, but He humbled Himself and took upon Himself the form

of a servant. He said that a seed must be placed in the ground and must die to itself before it could bear fruit. He taught that the way up is down. On the night before He died, He was not thinking of Himself, but others. He took a towel, girded Himself, and washed the feet of His disciples. This was a tremendous example of pure humility. He was simply teaching that if the Lord of Heaven could do a thing like this, surely His servants upon earth should be willing to do the same thing. Now "foot-washing" is not a church ordinance. It was not practiced by the New Testament churches. Paul and the other writers did not mention it. Some people practice this rite as an ordinance, saying that they are thus showing their humility. But a true humility does not have to be shown.

The cross was His greatest shame, but He did not shrink from it. He humbly went to His death and by that death He lifted the cross up to a position of dignity and honor.

II. The Meaning of Humility

1. *Humility is not a cringing, fawning attitude.* Dickens gave us a picture of Uriah Heep, washing his hands with invisible soap, and telling us always how "umble" he was. Jesus never cringed, although He was the humblest man who ever lived. We can be strong in the face of the world, yet in our hearts we can be the humblest of men.

2. *Humility is not self-deprecation.* Some people are always "throwing off" upon themselves. They say, "I am not clever, I am not talented, I am not this or that." This is not humility. This is simply false pride. The story is told of a Grecian philosopher who clothed himself in rags to show his humility. But the people said that they could see his pride peeking through the holes of his garments.

3. *Humility is a modest estimation of one's self.* The Pharisee said, "God, I thank thee, that I am not as other men are . . . or even as this publican" (Luke 18:11). He had the wrong estimate of himself. His estimation was too high. You have probably heard the expression, "If I could buy that man for what he is worth and sell him for what he thinks he is worth, I could be a rich man."

When most people compare themselves with others they pick

out some inferior character. They never pick out a big, fine Christian. They pick out one whose religion doesn't go very deep and never a spirit-filled man who is trying to do what God would have him do. The humble man will never say, "I am just as good as anybody else," but he will say, "Everybody else is certainly as good as I am or even better."

You can always find something bad in others which is not in yourself, but that is no excuse for wrong-doing on your part. You may say, "I do not lie as does this other man." But that does not excuse you from paying your bills. You say, "I pay my bills better than other men," but that does not excuse you from cursing. You may say, "I do not curse like other men," but that does not excuse you from gossiping. There is only one standard by which we are to judge ourselves, and that standard is Jesus. How do you stand when you measure yourself by Him?

A man may feel that he has reached a tremendous altitude when he stands on top of a mountain three thousand feet high. But if that mountain were placed by another mountain which is fourteen thousand feet high, this man would feel his inadequacy. In like manner you may "stack up" all right when measured by some sorry man, but how do you stand when you are measured by Jesus Christ? When we are tempted to feel proud of ourselves, we need to look to Jesus and to the great Christians of the ages. Then we are bound to say, "I thought I was doing quite well, but compared to them, I see how much bigger and better and more loving I could have been."

Some people will go to hell because they are not willing to humble themselves before God and ask forgiveness for their sins. Spurgeon tells of a bird who flew into his church. This bird flew high up around the dome of the church and could not find an exit. He beat himself against the windows until finally he dropped to the floor. Then he saw before him an open door and flew out to safety. That is like many a man. In his pride he says, "I am not a bad man. I can be saved by my own goodness." But there is no salvation in such an attitude. When finally he drops down to the floor of repentance he finds the door open and he makes his way to Jesus.

A prominent man applied for a position of service and the position was given to him. One day a friend heard him praying, "Take me out of myself. Don't let me be so uplifted that I will not be able to do my duty. God help me to be humble." Every Christian ought to pray that prayer.

One day a fisherman came upon an old man who was catching many trout. He said to him, "How can you catch so many fish when others are not catching them? What are your rules?" And the man said, "The first rule is to keep out of sight, the second rule is to keep farther out of sight, and the third is to keep even farther out of sight." If we are to catch men for Christ it would be good for us to learn that lesson, also. In the old days when I preached in the country churches I often heard men pray a prayer like this, "God bless our preacher, and help him to hide behind the cross so that we will see nothing else but Jesus and Him crucified." That is a good prayer and ought to be prayed by every preacher and every Christian worker.

One day Benjamin Franklin went to a neighbor's house and when his visit was over this neighbor showed him a short way out of the house. However, a low beam obstructed his pathway, so the neighbor cried out, "Stoop, stoop!" But it was too late, so Franklin bumped his head. The neighbor called him back and said, "Young man, when you go through the world, if you will stoop more often, you will not bump your head so many times." This thought stuck in Franklin's heart and he said that many times when pride assailed him and he thought that he was a big somebody, he remembered to stoop.

Let us learn to stoop. Let us not be exalted in our own opinion, but let us put Christ and others first. Then we will not have to shout it from the housetops. People will see our humility and know that we belong to Jesus.

15.

The Marks of a Christian — Separation

Galatians 6:17;
II Corinthians 6:17

We have been talking about the marks of a Christian, marks which he should bear in his life and character. We have thought about loyalty, courage, patience and humility. Now let us think about the matter of separation. What do we mean by separation? We do not mean an overly pious, holier-than-thou attitude. We do mean that when a man comes to Christ he should separate himself from evil and questionable things and be separated unto the Lord Jesus. His body should no longer be dedicated to the flesh, but to the things of the spirit. Old things are to pass away and all things are to become new.

I. SOME EXAMPLES OF SEPARATION

1. *Paul.* Before his conversion he was a Pharisee of the Pharisees. He was lined up with a group who considered the letter of the law the most important thing in all the world. Paul carried out the Mosaic law and all the traditions, but in doing so his heart became cold and dead. He served God with his lips but his heart was far from Him. He kept the law, but he consented to the murder of Christians. It was a religion of the head and not of the heart, a religion of the lips and not of the life. But one day Paul had a great experience. He met Jesus on the Damascus Road. He was converted and regenerated, made over by the transforming power of Christ. From that time on he was a changed man. He separated himself from the old life and the old ways. He fellowshiped with different people and went to different places. He served another Master. He was separated from the world and unto Jesus Christ. He still loved the old group and longed for their salvation, but he was separated from their Pharisaic beliefs and their way of life.

93

2. *The prodigal son.* There was a time when he went out into sin and spent his substance in riotous living. He lusted for the things of this world. But one day he came to himself and said, "I am through with this wicked life. It has brought me nothing but despair and hunger. I will go home to my father and to my father's house." Yonder he goes ragged, hungry, weary. As he tops the last hill overlooking his home, he sees his father running toward him. The father runs to meet him, gives him a kiss of welcome, puts the new robe upon him, and prepares a feast in his honor. Now he is separated from all the old life. He associates with different people, he eats at a different table, he lives in a different home. All the world knows that he is separated. That is the way it should be with every child of God. When they come back from the far country of sin, everything in their lives ought to be different.

3. *The children of Israel.* Down in Egypt they were nothing but slaves, driven by the Egyptian lash. They lived from the flesh-pots of a heathen country. And then Moses came to deliver them. He was a man sent from God. He led them out of Egypt and his successor, Joshua finally led them to the Promised Land. In that land they were no longer slaves, they were free. They no longer craved the leeks and the garlic of Egypt, for they had eaten manna from heaven. They were no longer in a heathen land, they were in God's chosen land. They had had a tremendous experience with God and now they were a separated people.

Their sin lay in the fact that they did not continue to live separated lives. They went far away from God and into idolatry and God was forced to punish them because of it. But their leaving Egypt and going to Canaan is an example of separation. Oh, when we meet Jesus Christ, we, too, are to leave the Egypt of sin and enter into the Canaan of a consecrated Christian life!

4. *Jesus.* If you want to see the most wonderfully separated man who ever lived you have only to look at the God-Man, Christ Jesus. He never sinned, He needed no regenerating experience, but He lived a life of complete separation from the world. He was separate from all sin, even the appearance of evil. He walked among sinful people, but His soul walked the clean heights with God. He never went to a place that was

wrong. He never did a wrong thing. He was never associated with evil. Oh, if we want to be like Him, we must bear in our bodies the marks of separation! He was in the world, but not of the world. That must also be true of every Christian.

II. WHAT ARE WE TO BE SEPARATED FROM?

1. *We are to be separated from sinful companions.* Many a man has started out in a fine way in the Christian life, but soon he went back to his sinful companions and drifted into sin. Oh, when Jesus comes into your heart, you ought to say, "Good-by, my sinful friends, I can walk no longer with you. I am going to travel with Jesus. Won't you come with me?" Surely we ought to use every influence at our command to win our former companions to Christ, but we should never go back with them into sin. We are not to be "unequally yoked together with unbelievers."

It is probable that if you decide to live a separated life, you will be forced to give up some of your former friends. But in their place you will have Jesus Christ, the best friend in all the world, and you will also have friendship with the best people in all the world. Our love for Christ ought to be so strong that we will be willing to give up anything for His sake.

2. *We are to be separated from sinful occupations.* If our occupations stand between us and the Lord, we ought to do something about it. If your occupation causes you to sin and desecrate the Lord's Day, you ought to seek another occupation. The Christian should be willing to cast everything aside and hold on to the Saviour.

A man who owned a saloon attended a revival meeting with his wife. He came under deep conviction for sin, but he said to his wife, "If I become a Christian I would be forced to give up my saloon and my good living." Then she asked him, "How much do you think you will make out of the saloon in the years that you have left?" And he replied, "I imagine it will be about $40,000." Then she said, "Isn't your soul worth more than that? Are you willing to give up heaven and go to hell for the sake of $40,000?" The man saw the point, closed up his saloon and gave his heart to the Saviour.

3. *We are to be separated from sinful places.* You can walk into some places as a sinner where you cannot walk as a Chris-

tian. The conscience which is really and truly regenerated will say, "I cannot go now to that place of sin." The real Christian will feel out of place in the sinful haunts of his former days.

There is an old story of a certain man who came often to town and hitched his horse near a saloon. He would then go into the saloon and have his drink. Then he was gloriously converted to Christ. However, when he came to town he still tied his horse to the same old hitching post near the saloon, although he did not go in and drink. An older and mature Christian shook his head and said, "That's a dangerous thing. He is staying too close to the saloon." The time came when the man went back to drinking. He had not fully separated himself from the sinful places which he frequented before his conversion. We don't know when Jesus will return. That is one reason why we should keep out of sinful places. We would not want Him to find us there.

4. *We are to be separated from sinful habits.* Yes, if a man's Christianity means anything, he must break off with the sinful habits which formerly gripped him. He will find that he has a fight on his hands. The devil will sometimes get him down, but he must not stay there. He must arise in the strength of the Lord and continue the good fight.

III. WHY SHOULD WE SEPARATE OURSELVES FROM THE WORLD?

1. *Because Jesus demands it.* He said, ". . . come out from among them, and be ye separate . . ." (II Corinthians 6:17). He knows what is best for us. He knows that as long as we hold on to sin we are in danger, so He calls us out to a separate life. If we love Him, His slightest wish will be our command. We are to say to Him, "Lord, what is Thy will in this matter?" And when He gives the answer we must say, "I will walk in Thy way."

2. *Because our influence depends upon it.* Influence is one of the mightiest things in the Christian life. All of us have an influence, either for good or bad. We are lifting men up or we are carrying them down. Most of the influence is an unconscious one. We do not know that we are exerting that influence, but someone is always watching us and being influenced by our lives. So let's use our influence for Christ. Let us so live that those who imitate us will rise to the highest and best.

Your influence cannot be for Christ unless you are separated from the world. This includes not only Sunday, but every day in the week. You cannot go out into the world of sin and keep your influence strong. Neither can you keep your life pure and clean. A man and his daughter once were discussing the matter of influence. She wanted to do something which her father thought would be questionable. He picked up a piece of coal and put it in her hand and then told her to put the coal down. When she did she saw the smutty marks upon her hand. Then the father said, "You see, if you go out into the world and do the things that are wrong they will leave their mark upon you." Our influence depends upon our good lives. We must keep them unspotted before the world.

A man who had just been saved and who had joined the church was asked who led him to Christ. He said that he picked out one man in the church and watched him for a year. He wanted to learn if this man lived a consistent Christian life. He said, "Thank God, the man stood the test. The influence of his good life brought me to Christ." If someone picked you out and watched your conduct for a year, what would be your influence upon him?

3. *Because our power depends upon it.* You will have no power with God or man if you are not living a separated life. And, oh, how we do need power! We need power in the face of the high and holy duties of life. We must come to God for that power and there will be no power for us if there is anything standing between us and the Saviour. Here are two mighty locomotives standing side by side. One can pull tons of power, while the other cannot pull an ounce. The answer lies in the fact that there is power in one locomotive and not in the other. Here are two Christians. One has no influence, but the other has a mighty influence for God. This man has the power because he has no sin standing between him and God.

A layman in a prayer meeting quoted the text, "What must I do to be saved?" To give emphasis to the question, he repeated it several times. And one of his neighbors spoke up and said, "Go and pay John Williams for that yoke of oxen." This illustrates the fact that a man may talk all right about spiritual things, but he will have no power over men unless his life is right before God and man.

One of the classes of Yale had a reunion thirty years after graduation. On one occasion the men met a nice looking young man whom they had never seen before. However, they were quick to say to him, "You must be the son of So-and-So, because you are the image of what he was thirty years ago." You see, the son had reproduced the father. Are we reproducing Christ in our lives? Do we look like Him? Are we bearing the marks of the Lord Jesus? Let us be separated from the things of the world and then men can say, "He is a true Christian."

16.

The Marks of a Christian — Generosity

Galatians 6:17;
Acts 20:35

We come now to speak of generosity, which is the sixth mark of a Christian. Some people think only of money when a preacher speaks of generosity and they shy away from a message on this subject. But generosity includes more than making a liberal gift. A man may be very liberal in giving to some cause, yet he may not have a very generous feeling in his heart. He may give more than a tithe, and yet not have the spirit of the Lord Jesus Christ.

A man gives a million dollars to some cause and people say he is generous. But he may not be a forgiving man and therefore we would not call him generous. If he is really generous, his generosity will go farther than his gift. It will go to his heart and he will be generous in forgiveness, also. Generosity must extend to the pocketbook, of course, but it must go farther. It must permeate all of a man's feelings and dealings.

What is generosity? It is the act of doing more than is expected of you. When you do only that which is expected you have done nothing. When you do more, you have been generous. When you tithe you do that which is expected of you. When you go beyond that you may be called generous. Jesus said that even thieves loved one another, for that is expected of them. It is expected of you that you love your own folks. But when you go out in love to those who despitefully use you, you are being generous in love.

I. EXAMPLES OF GENEROSITY

1. *Paul.* He was a strict Pharisee caring for no one but himself and his own narrow beliefs. But after Jesus had transformed his life, his heart was opened to all men. He ministered to all

99

classes. In one city they stoned him and left him for dead, but later he came back to minister to these same people. This was indeed an act of generosity. He said that he was "made all things to all men. . ." (I Corinthians 9:22). He was so generous-hearted that he would do anything necessary to win people to Christ. To the slaves he became a slave, to the prisoners he became a prisoner. Like his Master he generously gave of himself to others.

2. *The Good Samaritan.* You remember how the Jew went down to Jericho and how he fell among thieves and was wounded and robbed. The Levite and the Priest passed him by, but the Good Samaritan saved his life and took care of him. The Samaritan was supposed to be a man who hated the Jews, but he showed his generosity by his loving attitude toward this man. He put aside all hatred and generously gave himself to the man who hated him. He had the right spirit.

3. *Jesus.* There was no narrowness nor prejudice in Him. He looked with love upon Jew and Gentile, rich and poor, bond and free. He saw their needs and responded to them. He gave Himself generously to everyone. Let a man be in need and no matter what his country or his creed, Jesus stopped to help him. Let a sinful woman cry out — others may stone her, but Jesus lifted her up and helped her to the better life. See Him as He goes to the cross. He could have called down legions of angels to rescue Him, but instead He goes all the way to the cross, giving, giving, giving. He gave His time, His life, His love, His blood. If you are to follow Him, you must bear the mark of generosity.

II. To Whom Are We to Be Generous?

1. *To our friends and loved ones.* Sometimes we are most ungenerous to the ones we love the most. The meanest man in the world is the one who is generous downtown and stingy and pinching at home. He generously overlooks the faults of his business associates, but snaps like a dog at anyone who disturbs the peace in his home. The Bible tells us that a man who will not provide for his own household is worse than an infidel. He is not a Christian, surely. We should be even a little more generous in the home overlooking the faults of others as we would like for them to overlook ours.

2. *To our enemies.* It is hard to be generous to those who hurt us, but this is the biggest test of Christianity. When you learn to forgive quickly those who wrong you, you are manifesting the spirit of Christ. Jesus said, "Love your enemies, bless them that curse you, do good to them that hate you, and pray for them which despitefully use you, and persecute you" (Matthew 5:44). When you learn to do that, the world will know that you have the spirit of Christ in you. On the cross He prayed for His enemies, saying, "Father forgive them for they know not what they do. . ." (Luke 23:34). Can you offer a prayer like that for your enemies?

A slave owner was beating his Christian slave. In his anger he said to the slave, "What can Jesus Christ do for you now?" And the slave answered, "Master, He teaches me to forgive you." Oh, that's the spirit that we need!

Edwin M. Stanton was one of Lincoln's bitterest enemies. On one occasion he said, "If we want a gorilla for president, why don't we send to Africa for one?" But when Lincoln wanted a secretary of war, he appointed Stanton to the position for he felt that he was well qualified for it. This generosity so won the heart of Stanton that when Lincoln died, Stanton said, "There is the greatest ruler of men the world has ever known."

3. *To our rivals.* Two businessmen had stores across the street from each other. However, they disliked each other and would not speak to one another. One man was a Christian and he wanted to do the right thing. He took the matter to his pastor and his pastor said to him, "The way to win him is to send some of your customers over to his store when you cannot supply their needs." The man took this advice. When someone came to him for an article that he did not have in stock, he sent them across the street. This generosity on his part melted the heart of the other man and they became good friends.

We can have our own doctrinal and denominational beliefs, but we can still be generous with those who do not believe as we do. We are not the only ones who are going to heaven. Sometime ago a man said to one of my friends, "You cannot go to heaven if you remain in the church where you are now." And my friend answered, "What about your mother? She was a member of our church before she died." We can be firm in our beliefs, but we don't have to be so narrow that we believe everyone is lost who doesn't believe as we do.

4. *To outsiders.* Some people may not be as well educated as you are. Are you generous enough to overlook their mistakes? A college professor once heard Dwight L. Moody preach. After the service, he came up and said, "Mr. Moody, you made thirty-eight mistakes in English in your message." And Mr. Moody humbly said, "Yes, I know that I make many mistakes. I do not have as good an education as you do. However, I am using all of my education for the glory of God. Are you doing that?"

Nathaniel was not a very generous man when he first heard about Christ. He asked the question, "Can there any good thing come out of Nazareth? . . ." (John 1:46). He was not generous enough to know that there might be someone of worth in another town. We are to be generous to all men, realizing that God made them all and that Christ shed His blood for them all.

III. Why Ought We to Be Generous?

1. *Because God has been so generous to us.* What do we have which has not come from Him? He has poured out His blessings generously upon us. What would we do if He removed His hand for one second? Throughout the ages God has been bequeathing legacies to us, gifts of health, knowledge and power.

A Christian doctor was ministering to a young man and he asked him if he was a Christian. The young man replied, "No, doctor, I don't believe in that stuff." And the doctor answered, "It's a good thing that someone believed. You are getting well and you are going to live because you have some good blood in your veins, blood which you received from good people who lived for God." We have what we have today because God and others have bequeathed it to us. God has been generous with us and we ought to be generous in return. ". . . freely ye have received, freely give" (Matthew 10:8).

Jesus tells a story of a man who was forgiven a debt of ten million dollars, yet he would not forgive a debt of seventeen dollars. This was not generosity. God has forgiven us so much, in turn we ought to be generous with our forgiveness.

2. *Because we are stewards.* A steward is a man who holds property in trust for another. If a steward is honest, he does not use this property for himself, but he uses it rightly for the owner. All that we have belongs to God. We are to be careful as to how we use these things as stewards. Someone says, "This is my money, I worked hard for it, and I will do with it as I please." That's the wrong attitude if you are a Christian. Why do we give to our church and to various causes that it represents? We do it because we are Christians and because we are stewards.

3. *Because of the good it does others.* Our generosity not only blesses others, but it sets them an example. A little boy went to church one day to hear a missionary whom he had heard sometime before. He said to the missionary, "I gave you five cents some time ago. Let me see what you have done with it." Some people are just that cheap and that narrow.

During the Crimean War one company had a soldier who was indeed a black sheep. Nothing that was done for him seemed to help him in any way. No punishment which was meted out to him changed him in the least. His captain told a superior officer about it, and this officer said, "Why don't you try generosity?" The captain did just that. He began to forgive the man for the wrong things he had done and it broke the man's heart. He soon became one of the best men in the company.

We ought to give ourselves and our money because of the help it will give others. Too many men are holding on to their possessions, forgetting that soon they must die and leave all. Let us be generous in doing good unto others and they will thank us for it through eternity.

4. *Because generosity makes you a better person.* It takes generosity to strengthen the soul. You cannot pour perfume from a bottle without getting a little of it upon yourself. What is the difference in the Dead Sea and the Sea of Galilee? The Dead Sea has no outlet; therefore it is a "dead" sea. The Sea of Galilee has an outlet, and thus it can bless mankind. If your life is clogged with selfishness, you are of no use to the world, and you will soon dry up and die.

A great Christian giver was asked the question, "How can you give so much?" And he answered, "As I shovel out, God shovels in. And God uses a bigger shovel than I do." Yes, generosity helps us.

Leonardo da Vinci had an enemy whom he hated very much. He decided to paint this man's face in the great picture, *The Last Supper*. So he painted that man's face as the face of Judas, the traitor. Then he tried to paint the picture of Christ, and he could not do it. Every effort failed. Soon he realized that the hatred in his soul was crippling his art. He painted out the face of the man and went and forgave his enemy. Then he was able to paint the picture of Jesus with power. Oh, it takes a generosity of soul to make one a bigger and better Christian!

This is the last of these little talks. I have told you about the marks of a Christian. You remember that on the Mount of Transfiguration there was a time when the disciples saw no one but "Jesus only." I plead with you to live before men in such a way that they will see these marks in you. Live in such a way that those who see you will think of "Jesus only."